S0-DZM-952

# HOW TO MAKE A NEW YORK WILL

*with forms*

# HOW TO MAKE A NEW YORK WILL

*with forms*

James L. Rogers
Mark Warda
Attorneys at Law

Sphinx Publishing
A Division of Sourcebooks, Inc.
Naperville, IL • Clearwater, FL

Copyright © 1998 and 1999 by James L. Rogers and Mark Warda
Cover design © 1998 by Sourcebooks, Inc.

All rights reserved. No part of this book may be reproduced in any form or by any electronic or mechanical means including information storage and retrieval systems—except in the case of brief quotations embodied in critical articles or reviews, or in the case of the exercises in this book solely for the personal use of the purchaser—without permission in writing from its publisher, Sourcebooks, Inc.

Second Edition, 1999

Published by: **Sphinx® Publishing, A Division of Sourcebooks, Inc.®**

Naperville Office
P.O. Box 372
Naperville, Illinois 60566
630-961-3900
FAX: 630-961-2168

Clearwater Office
P.O. Box 25
Clearwater, Florida 33757
727-587-0999
FAX: 727-586-5088

Interior Design and Production: Shannon E. Harrington and Amy S. Hall, Sourcebooks, Inc.

This publication is designed to provide accurate and authoritative information in regard to the subject matter covered. It is sold with the understanding that the publisher is not engaged in rendering legal, accounting, or other professional service. If legal advice or other expert assistance is required, the services of a competent professional person should be sought.

*From a Declaration of Principles Jointly Adopted by a Committee of the American Bar Association and a Committee of Publishers and Associations*

**Library of Congress Cataloging-in-Publication Data**

Rogers, James L.
    How to make a New York will : with forms / James L. Rogers, Mark Warda, 2nd ed.
        p.   cm.
    Includes index.
    ISBN 1-57248-095-5
    1. Wills--New York (State)--Popular works.     I. Warda, Mark.
II. Title
KFN5201.Z9R64   1999                                    98-54391
346.74705'4--dc21                                            CIP

Printed and bound in the United States of America.
Paperback — 10 9 8 7 6 5 4 3 2 1

# CONTENTS

# Using Self-Help
# Law Books

Whenever you shop for a product or service, you encounter various levels of quality and price. In deciding what product or service to buy, you make a cost/value analysis on the basis of your willingness to pay and the quality you desire.

When buying a car, you decide whether you want transportation, comfort, status, or sex appeal. Accordingly, you decide among such choices as a Neon, a Lincoln, a Rolls Royce, or a Porsche. Before making a decision, you usually weigh the merits of each option against the cost.

When you get a headache, you can take a pain reliever (such as aspirin) or visit a medical specialist for a neurological examination. Given this choice, most people, of course, take a pain reliever, since it costs only pennies; whereas a medical examination costs hundreds of dollars and takes a lot of time. This is usually a logical choice because rarely is anything more than a pain reliever needed for a headache. But in some cases, a headache may indicate a brain tumor, and failing to see a specialist right away can result in complications. Should everyone with a headache go to a specialist? Of course not, but people treating their own illnesses must realize that they are betting on the basis of their cost/value analysis of the situation, they are taking the most logical option.

The same cost/value analysis must be made in deciding to do one's own legal work. Many legal situations are very straight forward, requiring a simple form and no complicated analysis. Anyone with a little intelligence and a book of instructions can handle the matter without outside help.

But there is always the chance that complications are involved that only an attorney would notice. To simplify the law into a book like this, several legal cases often must be condensed into a single sentence or paragraph. Otherwise, the book would be several hundred pages long and too complicated for most people. However, this simplification necessarily leaves out many details and nuances that would apply to special or unusual situations. Also, there are many ways to interpret most legal questions. Your case may come before a judge who disagrees with the analysis of our authors.

Therefore, in deciding to use a self-help law book and to do your own legal work, you must realize that you are making a cost/value analysis and deciding that the chance your case will not turn out to your satisfaction is outweighed by the money you will save in doing it yourself. Most people handling their own simple legal matters never have a problem, but occasionally people find that it ended up costing them more to have an attorney straighten out the situation than it would have if they had hired an attorney in the beginning. Keep this in mind while handling your case, and be sure to consult an attorney if you feel you might need further guidance.

# INTRODUCTION

This book's intent is to give New York residents a basic understanding of the laws regarding wills, joint property and other types of ownership of property as they affect their estate planning. It is designed to allow those with simple estates to set up their affairs quickly and inexpensively, and to distribute their property according to their wishes.

It also includes information on appointing a guardian for minor children. This can be useful in avoiding bad feelings between relatives and in protecting the children from being raised by someone to whom you would object.

Chapters 1 through 5 explain the laws which control wills. Chapters 6 and 7 discuss living wills and anatomical gifts. Appendix A contains sample filled-in will forms. Appendix B contains blank will forms you can cut out or photocopy.

You can prepare your own will quickly and easily by using the forms out of the book, or by photocopying them, or you can retype the material on blank paper. The small amount of time it takes to do this can give you and your heirs the peace of mind of knowing that your estate will be distributed according to your wishes.

A surprising number of people have had their estates pass to the wrong parties because of a simple lack of knowledge. Before using any of the forms in appendix B, you should read and understand the previous chapters in this book.

In each example given you might ask, "What if my spouse dies first?" or "What if the children are grown?" and then the answer might be different. If your situation is at all complicated you are advised to seek the advice of an attorney. In many communities wills are available for very reasonable prices. No book of this type can cover every contingency in every case, but a knowledge of the basics will help you make the right decisions regarding your property.

# Basic Rules You Should Know 1

## What Is a Will?

A will is a document you can use to control who gets your property, who will be guardian of your children, and who will manage your estate.

## How a Will Is Used

Some people think a will avoids probate. It does not. A will is the document used in probate to determine who receives your property. It also appoints guardians and personal representatives.

If you wish to avoid probate you need to use methods other than a will, such as joint ownership, pay-on-death accounts or living trusts. We will discuss the first two of these later in this chapter. For publications on living trusts, you should check with your bookstore or the publisher of this book.

You may not need a will if you can successfully avoid probate with all of your property. However, everyone should have a will in case some property, which was forgotten or received just prior to death, does not avoid probate for some reason.

# A Spouse Can Elect against a Will

Under New York law, a surviving spouse may have the right not to accept the property they are given under your will but rather take what is called an *elective share*. This share is one-third of your net estate if you are survived by one or more issue or descendants (children, grandchildren, etc.) and one-half of your net estate if there are no descendants alive at the time of your death. This is the case no matter what your will states. Moreover, you can not avoid this rule by giving away your property during your life in the form of joint tenancies, revocable trusts or gifts made in contemplation of your death. New York has cleverly prevented people from making such lifetime transfers to defeat a spouse's right to elect against a will by calling them *testamentary substitutes* and by including their value in your estate.

The only real way that you can defeat your spouse's right of election is if your spouse releases this right as in a prenuptial or post-nuptial agreement. So if your desire is that your spouse not be able to claim the elective share, you should have a properly drawn agreement stating that your spouse releases this statutory right.

# A Spouse May Have Community Property Rights in Your Estate

New York is not a *community property state*. This means that New York does not have laws which treat property that you and your spouse acquire during your marriage as community property. If New York were to treat all your property acquired during marriage as community property, your spouse would be considered as a one-half owner of all such property.

While New York is not a community property state, New York does look at all personal property that you may have once acquired with your spouse in a community property state as community property. Therefore, if you once lived in a community property state (Arizona, California, Idaho, Nevada, New Mexico, Texas, Washington, or Wisconsin), all personal property acquired by you and your spouse in that community property state will continue to remain as community property after you move to New York. The end result is that upon your death, your spouse will be entitled to one-half of that community property. So if you have lived in other states before moving to New York, you should keep a record of which property was acquired before or after your move.

# JOINT TENANCY OVERRULES A WILL

Where a will gives property to one person but it is already in a joint account with another person, the will is ignored and the joint owner of the account gets the property. This is because the property in the account avoids probate and passes directly to the joint owner. A will only controls property that goes through probate. There are exceptions to this rule. If some money is put into a joint account only for convenience it might pass under the will, but if the joint owner does not give it up, it could take an expensive court battle to get it back.

EXAMPLES

☞ Bill's will leaves all his property to his friend, Mary. Bill dies owning a house jointly with his sister, Joan, and a bank account jointly with his son, Don. Joan gets the house. Don gets the bank account. His friend, Mary, gets nothing.

☞ Betty's will leaves half her assets to Ann and half her assets to George. Betty dies owning $1,000,000 in stock jointly with George and a car in her own name. Ann gets only a half interest in the car. George gets all the stock and half the car.

☞ John's will leaves all his property equally to his five children. Before going in the hospital he names his oldest son, Harry, as a joint owner of his accounts. John dies and Harry gets all of his assets. The rest of the children get nothing.

In each of these cases the property went to a person it probably shouldn't have because the decedent didn't realize that joint ownership overruled their will. In some families, this might not be a problem. Harry might divide up the property equally (and possibly pay a gift tax.) But in many cases, Harry would just keep everything and the family would never talk to him again.

## JOINT TENANCY AVOIDS PROBATE

While the above cases show how joint tenancy can defeat a person's estate plan, if used properly joint tenancy can help one avoid probate and simplify your estate.

EXAMPLES

☞ When Ed and Suzanne married they put all their property and bank accounts in joint tenancy. When either of them dies, the other will inherit all property without a probate.

☞ Ethel's only heir is her forty-year-old granddaughter. She lives in a retirement home and her only assets are her bank CDs. She names her granddaughter as joint owner on the CDs. When she dies, the granddaughter may go to the bank and cash them without a probate procedure.

## JOINT TENANCY IS RISKY

The above cases may make it appear that joint tenancy is the answer to all problems, but it often creates even more problems. If you put your real estate in joint ownership with someone, you cannot sell it or mortgage it without that person's signature. If you put your bank account in joint ownership with someone, they can take out all of your money.

EXAMPLES

☞ In the first example above, if Ed had a lot of property and Suzanne had none when they married, putting it in joint tenancy may make it look like a gift in the court of a divorce. If Ed kept it all in his own name, he might not lose it in a divorce.

☞ Alice put her house in joint ownership with her son. She later married Joe and moved in with him. She wanted to sell her house and to invest the money for income. Her son refused to sign the deed. She was in court for ten months getting her house back and the judge almost refused to do it.

☞ Alex put his bank accounts into joint ownership with his daughter Mary to avoid probate. Mary fell in love with Doug who was in trouble with the law. Doug talked Mary into "borrowing" $30,000 from the account for a "business deal" that went sour. Later she "borrowed" $25,000 more to pay Doug's bail bond. Alex didn't find out until it was too late that his money was gone.

# "TENANCY IN COMMON" DOES NOT AVOID PROBATE

In New York, there are three basic ways to own property: joint tenancy with right of survivorship; tenancy in common; and the estate by the entireties. Joint tenancy with right of survivorship means when one owner of the property dies, the survivor automatically gets the decedent's share. *Tenancy in common* means—when one owner dies that owner's share of the property goes to his or her heirs or beneficiaries under the will. An estate by the entireties is like joint tenancy with right of survivorship, but it only applies to a married couple.

EXAMPLES

☞ Tom and Marcia, who were not married, bought a house and lived together for twenty years. But the deed did not specify joint tenancy. When Tom died his bother inherited his half of the house and it had to be sold because Marcia could not afford to buy it from him.

☛ Lindsay and her husband Rocky bought a house. When Rocky suddenly died, Lindsay obtained full ownership of the house by filing a death certificate at the courthouse. That was because the deed to the house stated that they were husband and wife so presumably ownership was tenancy by the entireties.

# BANK ACCOUNTS IN TRUST FORM

One way of keeping bank accounts out of your estate and still retain control is to title them "In Trust For," "As Trustee For," or simply "For" and by naming a beneficiary. These are called *Totten Trusts* after the man who had to go to court to prove they were legal. By keeping your bank accounts in trust form, you have full control over your money during your lifetime in that you can make deposits and withdrawals. If at any time your designated beneficiary predeceases you or you decide to revoke your trust account, then the funds in your account go back to you as an individual free and clear of the trust. At the time of your death, the funds in your trust account vest in your beneficiary automatically and do not pass under your will.

EXAMPLE  ☛ Rich opened a bank account in the name of "Rich, in trust for Mary." If Rich dies, the money automatically goes to Mary. Prior to his death, Mary has no control over or knowledge of the account, and Rich can take Mary's name off the account at any time.

# SECURITIES AND MUTUAL FUNDS CAN BE REGISTERED IN TRUST FORM

A new law has been passed by over half the states which allows people to register their stock, bonds, mutual funds and other securities in trust form. If you own these types of investments you can keep them out of probate simply with this method.

Unfortunately, New York has not yet passed this law, but you can take advantage of it. If your mutual fund or brokerage account is with a company in one of the states which allow such registrations you can set up an account in trust form. Check with your broker or mutual fund. If they cannot offer trust accounts it would be worth changing to one who does.

# SOME PROPERTY MAY BE EXEMPT FROM YOUR WILL

If you die, either with or without a will, certain property that you own will be given to your surviving spouse or to your minor children if you do not leave a surviving spouse. This property is called an *exemption for the benefit of your family* and you can not avoid it by any provision in your will. It includes most of your household furnishings up to an aggregate value of $10,000; family personal items like books and pictures up to $1,000; any automobile which you own at death up to the value of $15,000; and, other money or personal property up to the value of $15,000.

You can not avoid this exemption from your estate with any provision in your will. The only way that it can be avoided, with respect to your spouse, is if your spouse relinquishes this right such as in a premarital agreement or a post marital agreement. Moreover, any such relinquishment must specifically mention that your spouse is relinquishing all rights to claim the exemption.

EXAMPLE ☛ Donna died leaving an automobile which she owned as tenancy in common with her surviving husband. Donna's executor claimed that the surviving husband could not claim Donna's one-half ownership interest of $6,000 in the car because even if it were considered exempt property, Donna's husband had executed a prenuptial agreement relinquishing all statutory interests in his wife's estate. The court disagreed, holding that Donna's ownership interest was exempt property and that since the prenuptial agreement did not specifically mention that Donna's husband had waived his right to claim the exemption, the husband did not relinquish his right. The result was that Donna's husband was entitled to Donna's one-half ownership interest of $6,000 as exempt property.

## GETTING MARRIED AUTOMATICALLY CHANGES YOUR WILL

If you get married after making your will and do not rewrite it after the wedding, your spouse gets a share of your estate as if you had no will unless you have a pre-nuptial agreement, or you made a provision for your spouse in the will or you stated in the will that you intended not to mention your prospective spouse.

EXAMPLE ☛ John made out his will leaving everything to his disabled brother. When he married Joan, an heiress with plenty of money, he didn't change his will because he still wanted his brother to get his estate. When he died Joan got his entire estate and his brother got nothing.

# RIGHTS OF CHILDREN BORN AFTER YOUR WILL

If you make a will and do not mention a child who is born after you sign that will, that child will nevertheless be considered a beneficiary of your will in New York. The share of your estate taken by the child born after you sign your will depends on whether you have provided for any other child in your will. If you have provided for a child or children in your will, the child born after you make your will is entitled to an equal share of all of the property which you have given to your child or children named in your will. If you have not named any child or children as beneficiaries in your will, then your child born after you make your will is entitled to his or her intestate share (the share such child would have received if you died without making a will).

The goal of this rule of law is to insure that children born after a will is signed are not prevented from sharing in your estate simply because you may have forgotten to add them to your will. So if you desire that no children born after you sign your will become a part of your will, you should consider adding a clause in your will that specifically states this.

# HOW YOUR DEBTS ARE PAID

One of the duties of the person administering an estate is to pay the debts of the decedent. Before an estate is distributed the legitimate debts must be ascertained and paid.

An exception is *secured debts*, these are debts that are protected by a lien against property, like a home loan or a car loan. In the case of a secured debt, the loan does not have to be paid before the property is distributed.

EXAMPLE

☛ John owns a $100,000 house with a $80,000 mortgage and he has $100,000 in the bank. If he leaves the house to his brother and the bank account to his sister then his brother would get the home but would owe the $80,000 mortgage.

What if your debts are more than your property? Today, unlike hundreds of years ago, people cannot inherit other peoples' debts. A person's property is used to pay their probate and funeral expenses first and if there is not enough to pay their debts then the creditors are out of luck. However, if a person leaves property to people and does not have enough assets to pay his or her debts then the property will be sold to pay the debts.

EXAMPLE ☞ Jeb's will leaves all of his property to his three children. At the time of his death Jeb has $30,000 in medical bills, $11,000 in credit card debt, and his only assets are his car and $5,000 in stock. The car and stock would be sold and the funeral bill and probate fees paid out of the proceeds. If any money was left it would go to the creditors and nothing would be left for the children. The children would not have to pay the medical bills or credit card debt.

## ESTATE AND INHERITANCE TAXES

If you die as a resident of New York state, you will be subject to a New York state estate tax if the adjusted value of your estate totals $108,333 or more. The tax is progressive which means that the more the value of your estate exceeds $108,333, the more tax you will owe. Decedents who are not residents of New York are also subject to this estate tax with respect to their real or personal property having an actual situs in New York.

There is a federal estate tax for estates above a certain amount. Estates below that amount are allowed a *unified credit* which exempts them from tax. The unified credit applies to the estate a person can leave at death and to gifts during his or her lifetime. In 1999, the amount exempted by the unified credit is $650,000 but it will rise to

$1,000,000 by the year 2006. The amount will change according to the following schedule.

| Year | Amount |
|------|--------|
| 1999 | $650,000 |
| 2000-2001 | $675,000 |
| 2002-2003 | $700,000 |
| 2004 | $850,000 |
| 2005 | $950,000 |
| 2006 | $1,000,000 |

# ANNUAL EXCLUSION

When a person makes a gift, that gift is subtracted from the amount entitled to the unified credit available to his or her estate at death. However, a person is allowed to make gifts of up to $10,000 per person per year without having these subtracted from the unified credit. This means a married couple can make gifts of up to $20,000 per person. The Taxpayer Relief Act of 1997 provided that this exclusion amount will be adjusted for inflation.

# DO YOU NEED A NEW YORK WILL? 2

## WHAT A WILL CAN DO

A will allows you to decide who gets your property after your death. You can give specific personal items to certain persons and decide which of your friends or relatives deserve a greater share of your estate. You can leave gifts to schools and charities.

A will allows you to decide who will be the executor (male) or executrix (female) of your estate. An executor or executrix is the person who gathers all your assets and distributes them to the beneficiaries. With a will you can provide that your executor or executrix does not have to post a surety bond with the court in order to serve and this can save your estate some money.

A will allows you to choose a guardian for your minor children. This way you can avoid fights among relatives and make sure the best person raises your children. You may also appoint separate guardians over your children and over their money. For example, you may appoint your sister as guardian over your children, and your father as guardian over their money. That way a second person could keep an eye on how their money was being spent.

You can set up a trust to provide that your property is not distributed immediately. Many people feel that their children would not be ready to handle large sums of money at the age of eighteen. A will can direct that the money is held until the children are twenty-one or twenty-five or older.

## WHAT IF YOU HAVE NO WILL?

If you do not have a New York will, New York law says that your property must be distributed as follows:

☞ If you are survived by a spouse and issue, $50,000 and one-half of the value of your estate beyond that amount will go to your spouse. Anything left over after your spouse's share is distributed goes to your issue by representation.

The term *issue* is defined as your descendants in any degree. Thus issue would include your children and grandchildren. The term *by representation* means that any of your estate allocated to your issue will be allocated in equal shares to your surviving issue who are in the generation closest to you as well as any issue in that generation who predeceased you but who also were survived by their own issue. For example, if you are survived by two children but also gave birth to a third child who predeceased you and who left his or her own issue, your estate would be divided into three shares. Two-thirds would be distributed to your two living children and the other one-third would be distributed to the issue of your predeceased child.

☞ If you are survived by your spouse and no issue, your spouse will take your entire estate.

☞ If you are survived by issue and no spouse, your estate will go to your issue by representation.

☞ If you are not survived by a spouse or any issue but are survived by one or both of your parents, your estate will go to your surviving parent or parents.

☞ If you are not survived by a spouse, any issue, or by any of your parents, your estate will go to the issue of your deceased parents by representation.

☞ If you are not survived by any of the above people, there are additional rules for the distribution of your estate to your grandparents or to the issue of your grandparents if you are not survived by grandparents. You should consult the Estates, Powers and Trusts Law §4-1.1 for the specific rules.

EXAMPLE ☞ Ebenezer dies without a will. Ebenezer was survived by two children, Tom and Joe. His wife and other two children, Anne and Rachelle had predeceased Ebenezer. However, Anne's two children and Rachelle's one child were living at the time of Ebenezer's death. Under New York law, Tom and Joe would inherit one-fourth each of Ebenezer's estate. The other one-half of his estate would be distributed evenly (one-sixth each) among Anne's two children and Rachelle's one child.

One more thing to note about dying without a will is that the probate of your estate can become more costly since there will be a need for court proceedings to determine who will be the administrator of your estate. An administrator has the same job as an executor if you leave a will appointing an executor. (As to your executor or executrix, see chapter 3.) There will also be a need for court proceeding to determine the guardian of any of your minor children.

# Is Your Out-of-State Will Valid in New York?

With respect to all of your personal property wherever it may be located, and with respect to all your real property located in New York, your out-of-state will is valid in New York even if it does not meet all the necessary procedures of New York for the valid signing of a will so long as the following is true. Your will must be in writing, signed by you and satisfy the laws of the state in which you signed your will, or else satisfy the laws of the state in which you were domiciled either at the time you signed your will or at the time of your death.

EXAMPLE

☞ Jerry executed his will in State X which did not require that a testator publish the will (make it known to the witnesses that the document which the testator was signing was a will). With the laws of State X in mind, Jerry did not publish his will and later died in New York, leaving real property in New York and personal property in several states. Even though the will would not be valid under the procedures which New York requires for a validly executed will since it was not published, a New York court would accept the will for probate in New York because it was still validly executed in State X where it was signed. Thus, Jerry's out-of-state will was valid in New York.

# Who Can Make a New York Will?

Any person who is eighteen or more years of age and of sound mind.

# What a Will Cannot Do

A will cannot direct that anything illegal be done and it cannot put unreasonable conditions on a gift. A provision that your daughter gets all of your property if she divorces her husband would be ignored by the court. She would get the property with no conditions attached. You can put some conditions in your will, to be sure they are enforceable, you should consult with an attorney.

A will cannot leave money or property to an animal because animals cannot legally own property. If you wish to care for an animal after your death you should leave it in trust or to a friend whom you know will care for the animal.

## Who Can Use a Simple Will?

The wills in this book will pass your property whether your estate is $1,000 or $100,000,000. However, if your estate is over $650,000 (this amount will rise to $1,000,000 by the year 2006) then you might be able to avoid estate taxes by using a trust or other tax-saving device. The larger your estate the more you can save on estate taxes by doing more complicated planning. If you have a large estate and are concerned about estate taxes you should consult an estate planning attorney or a book on estate planning.

## Who Should Not Use a Simple Will?

WILL CONTEST

If you expect that there may be a fight over your estate or that someone might contest your will's validity, you should consult a lawyer. If you leave less than the statutory share of your estate to your spouse or if you leave one or more of your children out of your will, it is likely that someone will contest your will.

COMPLICATED ESTATES

If you are the beneficiary of a trust or have any complications in your legal relationships, you may need special provisions in your will.

BLIND OR UNABLE TO WRITE

A person who is blind or who can sign only with an "X" should also consult a lawyer about the proper way to make and execute a will.

ESTATES OVER
$650,000

If you expect to have over $650,000 (this amount will rise to $1,000,000 by the year 2006) at the time of your death, you may want to consult with a CPA or tax attorney regarding tax consequences.

CONDITIONS

If you wish to put some sort of conditions or restrictions on the property you leave you should consult a lawyer. For example, if you want to leave money to your brother only if he quits smoking, or to a hospital only if they name a wing in your honor, you should consult an attorney to be sure that your conditions are valid in your state.

# How to Make a Simple Will 3

## Identifying Parties in Your Will

When making your will, it is important to correctly identify the persons you name in your will. In some families, names differ only by middle initial or by Jr. or Sr. Be sure to check the names before you make your will. You can also add your relationship to the party, and their location such as "my cousin, Richard Harris of Albany, New York" The same applies to organizations and charities. For example, there are more than one group using the words "cancer society" or "heart association" in their names. Be sure to get the correct name of the group you intend to leave your gift.

## Personal Property

Because people acquire and dispose of personal property so often, it is not advisable to list a lot of small items in your will. Otherwise, when you sell or replace one of them you may have to rewrite your will.

One solution is to describe the type of item you wish to give. For example, instead of saying, "I leave my 1998 Ford to my sister," you should say, "I leave any automobile I own at the time of my death to my sister."

Of course, if you do mean to give a specific item you should describe it. For example instead of "I leave my diamond ring to Joan," you should say, "I leave to Joan the one-half carat diamond ring which I inherited from my grandmother," because you might own more than one diamond ring at the time of your death. (Hopefully!)

# How to Make Testamentary Gifts

When you make gifts under your will (testamentary), you are said to *bequeath* personal property and to *devise* real property. For example, if you wanted to give your house to your daughter, you could state in your will "I devise my dwelling house and premises described as 201 Washington Avenue, Albany, New York to my daughter, Anne Huges, together with all policies of fire, burglary, property damage and other insurance thereon."

Bequests of personal property can be made in three ways. The first way is through a *specific* bequest in which you employ language that distinguishes the personal property that you are giving from all other property in your estate. To make a specific bequest, you should employ the word "my" before the property which you are giving away under your will. For example, if you state in your will "I give and bequeath to Anne Murray my 100 shares of IBM stock," you have made a specific bequest. On the other hand, if you were to state "I give and bequeath to Anne Murray 100 shares of IBM stock" without employing the word "my," you will have made a *general* instead of specific bequest. A third way to give away personal property is called a *demonstrative* bequest. A demonstrative gift is a mix between a specific and general bequest. When you make a demonstrative gift, you are making a general gift out of a specific part of your estate. The statement, "I give and bequeath the sum of $1,000 to be paid out of the proceeds of the sale of a sufficient number of my IBM stock," would be a demonstrative gift.

While the differences between specific, general, and demonstrative gifts of your personal property may seem minute, these different types of bequests have significance in the law. You should first note that when you make a specific bequest of property, that property will only go to your designated beneficiary under the terms of your will if such property exists in your estate at the time of your death. Thus if you make a specific bequest of "100 shares of my IBM stock," there must be IBM shares of stock for your beneficiary to be able to take any such shares. If you have sold this particular stock prior to your death, the gift is said to *adeem* and your beneficiary would not inherit anything under your will. By making your gift specific, the law says that those specific shares of IBM stock must exist on the date of your death. On the other hand, if you make a general or demonstrative bequest of the same 100 shares, your beneficiary would still be able to inherit the value of 100 shares of IBM stock even if these specific shares had previously been sold prior to your death. This is true because general and demonstrative bequests are paid out of the general assets of your estate.

With respect to the consequence of specific, general and demonstrative bequests, there is a second point that you should note: If the assets in your estate are not large enough to satisfy all of the administrative expenses and gifts under your will, general bequests will be used to meet these liabilities before demonstrative and specific gifts unless you provide otherwise in your will. Thus, if you are concerned that your estate will not be large enough to meet all of your bequests in your will, and you desire, for example, that your daughter take her bequest at the expense of your bequest to your personal friend, Tom, you would need to add a provision in your will like "in the event that my estate shall prove insufficient to pay my bequests provided herein in full, I direct my executor to apply my estate first to the payment in full of the bequest to my daughter and second to the payment of my bequest to my friend, Tom."

One last point: your beneficiary will take not only any property that you devise or bequeath, but also and any liens to which the property is subject, unless you provide otherwise in your will. For example, if you devise your residence to your spouse, that residence will be subject to any mortgages that still exist on the property. A way to provide otherwise in your will would be to state "if at the time of my death, the devise of my residence to my spouse shall be subject to any lien, security interest, or other charge, the same shall be paid out of my residuary estate and the said devisee shall receive the same free and clear of any such lien." Of course by making such a statement, you must realize that other beneficiaries under your residuary estate would have to give up their inheritance to pay off any such mortgage.

## RESIDUARY CLAUSE

A *residuary clause* is the clause in your will by which you name one or more persons to take all "the rest and residue" of your estate. Any time that you make testamentary gifts in your will to specific persons, you should also include a residuary clause to dispose of any other property which you may own at the time of your death. If you do not include a residuary clause, any property which you have not specifically given away under the terms of your will falls into intestacy.

EXAMPLE ☞ Bob created a will leaving all of his "earthly belongings" to his wife with no provision covering the situation where his wife predeceased him. Bob died after the death of his wife, and he had not changed his will. All of Bob's property passed outside his will according to the laws of intestacy. Bob could have avoided this problem by providing for a substituted beneficiary and by using a residuary clause.

Wills often make specific gifts of a testator's property and then include a residuary clause in which the bulk of the testator's estate goes to close relatives. One important thing to keep in mind when creating such a will is the possibility that your estate may decline in value. This may result in your specific testamentary gifts taking up a large proportion of your estate and leaving little or no property to your close relatives under the residuary clause. To counteract this problem, it is advisable to use percentages or fractions when making bequests of your property to insure that the persons named in your residuary clause inherit the largest portion of your estate.

EXAMPLE ☞ At the time Anne made her will, her estate was worth $300,000. Anne wanted very much to give each of her three nieces $15,000 and to give the rest of her estate to her two children so Anne created a will specifically giving her three nieces $15,000 each and gave the "rest, residue and remainder" of her estate to her children. At the time of Anne's death, her estate was worth only $45,000 due to unexpected health care costs. Under the terms of her will, each of the three nieces would inherit $15,000 leaving no property to pass to her children. Anne could have avoided this problem by giving each of her three nieces five percent or one-twentieth of her estate in which case her three nieces would have taken only $2,250 of her estate with the remaining $38,250 to be divided among her children.

If you feel compelled to make specific testamentary gifts of a certain dollar value rather than by using fractions or percentages, you should remember to make changes to your will if your assets change.

## Alternate Beneficiaries

You should always provide for an *alternate beneficiary* in case the person you name dies before you and you do not have a chance to make out a new will. If you do not the gift is said to *lapse*. In such a case, New York's *anti-lapse statute* kicks in and determines who gets the property.

SURVIVOR OR DESCENDANTS
Suppose your will leaves your property to your sister and brother; however, your brother predeceases you. Should his share go to your sister or to your brother's children or grandchildren?

If you are giving property to two or more persons and you want it all to go to the other if one of them dies, you would specify "or the survivor of them."

If, on the other hand, you want the property to go to the children of the deceased person, you should state in your will "or their lineal descendants." This would include his or her children and grandchildren.

FAMILY OR PERSON

If you decide you want it to go to your brother's children and grandchildren, you must next decide if an equal share should go to each family or to each person. For example: your brother leaves three grandchildren, one is an only child of his daughter and the others are the children of his son. Should all grandchildren get equal shares or should they take their parent's share?

When you want each family to get an equal share it is called *per stirpes*. When you want each person to get an equal share it is called *per capita*. Most of the wills in this book use per stirpes because that is the most common way property is left. If you wish to leave your property per capita then you can rewrite the will with this change.

EXAMPLE

☛ Alice leaves her property to her two daughters, Mary and Pat in equal shares, or to their lineal descendants per stirpes. Her daughter, Pat, predeceases Alice, leaving two children. Mary would receive one half of the estate and Pat's two children will receive the other half of the estate. In this case, if had Alice chosen per capita, Mary and the grandchildren would have each received one third of the estate.

## Per Stirpes Distribution

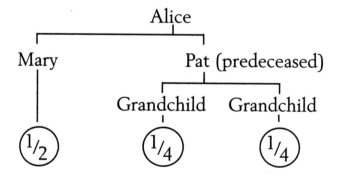

## Per Capita Distribution

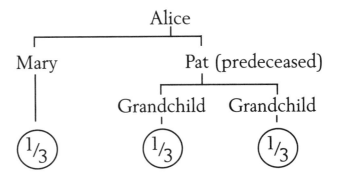

There are fourteen different forms in this book, but you may want to divide your property slightly differently from what these forms state. If so, you can re-type the forms according to these rules, specifying whether the property should go to the survivor or the lineal descendants. If this is confusing to you, consider seeking the advice of an attorney.

# SURVIVORSHIP

Many people put a clause in their will stating that anyone receiving property under the will must survive for thirty days (or forty-five or sixty) after the death of the deceased. This is so that if the two people die in the same accident there will not be two probates and the property will not go to the other party's heirs.

EXAMPLE

☛ Fred and Wilma were married and each had children by previous marriages. They didn't have survivorship clauses in their wills and they were in an airplane crash. Fred's children hired several expert witnesses and a large law firm to prove that at the time of the crash Fred lived for a few minutes longer than Wilma. That way when Wilma died first, all of her property went to Fred. When he died a few minutes later, all of Fred and Wilma's property went to his children and Wilma's children received nothing.

# GUARDIANS

If you have minor children you should name a guardian for them. There are two types of guardians, a guardian over the *person* and a guardian over the *property*. The first is the person who decides where the children will live and makes the other parental decisions for them. A guardian of the property is in charge of the minor's property and inheritance. In most cases, one person is appointed guardian of both the person and property. But some people prefer the children to live with one person, but to have the money held by another person.

EXAMPLE ☛ Sandra was a widow with a young daughter. She knew that if anything happened to her, her sister would be the best person to raise her daughter. But her sister was never good with money. So when Sandra made out her will, she named her sister as guardian over the person of her daughter and she named her father as guardian over the estate of her daughter.

When naming a guardian, it is always advisable to name an alternate guardian in case your first choice is unable to serve for any reason.

# CHILDREN'S TRUST

When a parent dies leaving a minor child and the child's property is held by a guardian, the guardianship ends when the child reaches the age of 18 and all of the property is turned over to the child. Most parents do not feel their children are competent at the age of 18 to handle large sums of money and prefer that it be held until the child is 21, 25, 30 or even older.

If you wish to set up a complicated system of deciding when your children should receive various amounts of your estate, you should consult a lawyer to draft a trust. However, if you want a simple provision that you want the funds held to a higher age than 18, and you have someone you trust to make decisions about paying for education or other expenses for your child or children, you can put that provision in your will as a children's trust.

The children's trust trustee can be the same person as the guardian or a different person. It is advisable to name an alternate trustee if your first choice is unable to handle it.

# YOUR EXECUTOR OR EXECUTRIX

An *executor* is the person who will be in charge of your probate. When your designated executor is a female, she is called your *executrix*. You may appoint more than one executor or executrix of your will. Your choice of an executor/executrix is perhaps the most significant decision you'll make in your will. He or she will gather your assets, handle the sale of them if necessary, prepare an inventory, hire an attorney and distribute the property. Any person who is not under eighteen, incompetent or a felon is eligible to be your executor. Some possible choices include a beneficiary under your will, your attorney, or a close friend. In any case, you should choose a person you trust. You should also be aware that whoever you choose as an executor is entitled to payment (called a *commission*) for their services which is paid directly out of your estate.

Some people like to name two persons as executors to avoid jealously or because they may want one of their executors who is skilled in business matters to serve along with another who lacks such skills. However, you should be aware that this can be time-consuming when it comes time to probate your estate since both executors must sign all necessary papers and there can be problems if your executors do not agree on something.

It is recommended to provide that your executor does not have to post any bond in any jurisdiction for the faithful performance of his or her duties. Otherwise, a bond may be required to be posted.

If you neglect to appoint an executor in your will or your appointed executor/executrix fails to qualify for some reason, then the court must appoint someone to perform the duties of an executor. This person is referred to as an *administrator with the will annexed* or *administrator c.t.a.* for short. Only certain persons are eligible to apply for the position. If you are interested in learning about who can qualify, you should consult the Surrogate's Court Procedure Act §1418.

## WITNESSES

A will must be witnessed by two persons to be valid in New York. In Vermont, three witnesses are required, so if you own real property in Vermont you should have three witnesses to your will. In some states a will that is entirely handwritten is valid if there are no witnesses, but in New York even a handwritten will needs a witness.

It is a good idea to place before the signatures of your witnesses a clause which sets forth the performance of all the requirements to a validly executed will. This clause is called an *attestation clause* and is included in all the forms in this book.

The witnesses you choose to witness your will should not be any persons who are beneficiaries under your will. In other words, if you have given a person any property under your will, you should make sure that such a person does not serve as a witness to your will. While the witnessing by a person who is a beneficiary under your will does not invalidate your will, such a witness will not be able to take your property given to him under your will as you have intended.

## SELF-PROVING CLAUSE

Even if no person objects to the probate of your will after your death, a court will require that the two witnesses to your will come to court in order to be examined about the genuineness of your will and its proper execution. This procedure is called *proving the will*, and it can be time-consuming and costly since your witnesses must be located and various procedures must be followed if such witnesses can no longer be located or do not exist. However, if you have each of your two witnesses sign a clause, called a *self-proving clause*, before a notary public that your will was executed with all the required formalities, this sworn statement may be accepted by the court in place of the production of each of your attesting witnesses at the time of your death. The net result is to save your estate a lot of hassle and money.

## DISINHERITING SOMEONE

Because it may result in your will being challenged in court, you should not make your own will if you intend to disinherit someone. However, you may wish to leave one child less than another because you already made a gift to that child, or perhaps that child needs the money less than the other.

If you do give more to one child than to another, then you should state your reasons to show that you thought out your plan. Otherwise, the one who received less might argue that you didn't realize what you were doing and were not competent to make a will.

## FUNERAL ARRANGEMENTS

You have the right to determine the manner of burial of your body after your death. This right includes the right to be cremated. However, since your will may not be read until after your body has been buried, it is advisable to let your family know about your wishes. You should express your wishes clearly in the manner that you desire and insert this clause directly into your will. Here are two examples of possible clauses which could be inserted into your will.

*(1) I direct my funeral be conducted by _____ (name of funeral agency) according to the rites of the _____ (name of church), and that my remains be interred in the plot owned by me _____ (name of cemetery) in the county of _____ of New York,*

*(2) I direct that my body shall be cremated and that my ashes be disposed of as my wife shall deem fitting.*

# HANDWRITTEN WILLS

In some states, a will that is entirely handwritten (called a *holographic will*) is also valid, even if there are no witnesses, but in New York such a will is not valid unless witnesses are present.

# FORMS

There are fourteen different will forms included in this book for easy use. You can either cut them out or photocopy them, or you can retype them on plain paper.

The forms in this book are printed on both sides of the page. If you photocopy them on separate pages or type your will on more than one piece of paper you should staple the pages together, initial each page and have both witnesses initial each page and each page should state at the bottom, "page 1 of 3," "page 2 of 3," etc.

# CORRECTIONS

Your will should have no white-outs or erasures. If for some reason it is impossible to make a will without corrections, they should be initialed by you and both witnesses.

# How to Execute a Will 4

The signing of a will is a serious legal event and must be done properly or the will may be declared invalid. Preferably, it should be done in a private room without distraction. All parties must watch each other sign and no one should leave the scene until all have signed.

EXAMPLE ☞ Phil brought over a folded document and told his good friends that it was his will and that he needed his friends to be witnesses. The friends agreed and signed in the appropriate blank spaces but never saw Phil sign his will. After Phil's death, the surrogate court refused to probate Phil's will because the witnesses testified that they had never actually seen Phil sign his will. Phil's property passed to persons not named in his will through the law of intestacy.

PROCEDURE After reading the will you (the testator) should assemble at least two witnesses who will not be beneficiaries under your will. You should state, "This is my will. I have read it and I understand it and this is how I want it to read. I want you two people to be my witnesses." You should next read the attestation clause (the clause just above the blanks where the witnesses sign) out loud. You must next date and sign your name at the end of the will in full view of the witnesses. You must next request that the witnesses sign their respective names and addresses below your signature.

After your witnesses have signed as attesting witnesses under your name, it is highly recommended that you have the witnesses sign an affidavit with a *self-proving clause*. As already discussed, this will enable the will to be probated at the time of your death without having to bring your witnesses to court. In order to properly complete the affidavit, you will need each of your attesting witnesses to sign the affidavit before a notary public. The notary public should not be one of your two witnesses.

It is a good idea to make at least one copy of your will, but you should not personally sign or notarize the copies. The execution of copies of your will can create problems for your estate. For example, the loss of one of the executed copies of a will creates a presumption that possibly you destroyed your will. This possibility prevents the probate of the will because of the lack of proof that you did not intend to destroy your will.

You should be very careful executing (signing) copies of your will. The safest policy is to keep only one will that has been signed by you. By executing more than one copy of your will, you may needlessly create a court battle over whether you have revoked your will.

EXAMPLE  ☞  Ed typed up his will in triplicate consisting of a ribbon copy and two carbon copies. Ed executed all three copies of the will, keeping the two carbon copies at his home and the one ribbon copy at his attorney's office. Upon Ed's death, no one could locate the carbon copies at Ed's home. A large court battle subsequently ensued over whether Ed's ribbon copy could be probated. Since the carbon copies were in Ed's exclusive control and could not be located, there was a presumption that Ed destroyed these copies and since all the executed copies constituted Ed's will, the court held that the revocation of any one of them revoked the other.

Ed could have avoided the subsequent battle over his will if he had executed only one copy of his will. If Ed had executed only one copy instead of the two others, the destruction of this one copy would have clearly shown his intention to revoke his will and there may not have been subsequent litigation over whether he intended to probate the executed copy held by his attorney. The lesson is the following: Unexecuted copies of your will are fine, but you should only store one copy of your will with your signature on it!

# After You Sign Your Will  5

## Storing Your Will

You should keep your will in a place safe from fire and easily accessible to your heirs. Your Executor should know of its whereabouts or you may risk that no one will discover your will after you die. You should note that if you decide to keep your will in a safe-deposit box that a court order will be required to obtain that will after your death.

Another possible place to keep your will is right with the surrogate court (the court which will be used to probate your will) in your county of residence. By statute, the surrogate court must accept your will for safekeeping, and the court will give you a receipt acknowledging that you have deposited your will with the court. However, before the court will accept your will, you must seal your will in an envelope and write the day, month and year that you have deposited your will on the sealed envelope. Although certain surrogate courts such as the one in Albany county do not charge a fee for storing your will, you need to check with the court of your county since a fee may be charged. After your death, the surrogate court will open your will and file it in the court.

# REVOKING YOUR WILL

Once you have made a will you may revoke it or may direct someone else to revoke it in your presence. This may be done by burning, tearing, cutting, cancellation, obliteration or by other mutilation or destruction of your will.

EXAMPLE
☞ Ralph tells his son Clyde to go to the basement safe and tear up his (Ralph's) will. If Clyde does not tear it up in Ralph's presence it is probably not effectively revoked.

You may also revoke your will by properly executing a will or codicil at a later time stating that you expressly revoke your earlier will. You should note that if you make a later will and do not include a clause expressly revoking your earlier will, your earlier will is not revoked. The first will's provisions will be effective to the extent that they are consistent with your new will.

If you need to revoke your will that is filed with the surrogate court, you need to physically go to the court and sign a log book. Make sure you bring identification and a sealed envelope with the name of the will, the date of the will, and the names of the witnesses. If you cannot go to surrogate court (for example, if you are in the hospital), then you can revoke your will by executing a new will which revokes it.

REVIVAL
What if you change your will by drafting a new one and later decide you don't like the changes and want to go back to your old will? Can you destroy the new one and revive the old one? NO! Once you execute a new will revoking an old one you cannot revive the old one unless you execute a new document stating that you intend to revive the old will. In other words, you might as well execute a new will.

# CHANGING YOUR WILL

You should not make any changes on your will after it has been signed. If you wish to change some provision of your will, you can do it by executing a document called a *codicil*. A person may make an unlimited number of codicils to a will, but each one must be executed with the same formality of a will and should be self-proved. Therefore, it is usually better to just prepare a new will than to prepare codicils. If you wish to prepare a codicil to your will, then you can use the form included in this book.

# EFFECT OF DIVORCE ON YOUR WILL

You should note that a divorce, annulment, declaration of nullity or dissolution of your marriage revokes any appointment of property made in your will to your former spouse as well as any provision naming your former spouse as an executor or trustee unless your will contains a provision stating that this result should not be the case. However, events like divorce do not invalidate your will. Your will is simply probated as though your former spouse predeceased you.

# HOW TO MAKE A LIVING WILL **6**

A *living will* is a document in which one states, while in good health, what measures he or she does not want used to extend one's life when one is dying. Although the New York Legislature has not yet adopted a statute recognizing the validity of a living will, New York courts have upheld your right to make such a document and to thereby decline certain medical treatment by artificial means and devices while in a terminally ill state or condition.

A form that you can use as a living will is included in appendix B. The execution of such a form by you is a personal decision. You can use this form or create your own form. In either case, you should be specific about what type of treatments you do not want should you reach a terminal state: The document will speak for you should you later be incompetent and in a terminal ill condition.

In order to properly execute a living will, you should sign the document in the presence of at least two witnesses eighteen years of age or older, who must also sign the document.

Related to the living will is a *health care proxy*. This document gives someone you designate the power to make medical or other health care decisions for you. Any competent adult can create a health care proxy by signing and dating the proxy in the presence of the two adult witnesses who must make these decisions either in accordance with your wishes or if such wishes are not reasonably known, then in accordance with your best interests. However, if your views regarding artificial nutrition and hydration are not reasonably known, then the agent will not have the authority to make those types of decisions. So you should expressly state your desires with respect to artificial nutrition and hydration in the proxy in order for your agent to act according to your wishes. Further information on health care proxies can also be found in the *New York Power of Attorney Handbook,* by William P. Coyle and Edward A. Haman published by Sourcebooks, Inc.

Another document which can be useful prior to your death is a *power of attorney.* Unfortunately, there can be months and often years prior to the time of your death where you may be unable to handle your affairs because of mental or physical disability. In a power of attorney, you can designate an agent to make just about any type of decision which you can make yourself. Moreover, so long as you state in the power of attorney that "this power of attorney shall not be affected by subsequent disability or incompetence of the principle," your agent can act on your behalf even during your incompetence. In the power of attorney, you can designate the particular powers which you want to confer upon your agent by initialing next to such powers contained in the form. More information on how to make a power of attorney is also contained in the *New York Power of Attorney Handbook.*

# How to Make Anatomical Gifts 7

Any person of sound mind who is eighteen years old or older can donate all or any part of his or her body for scientific research or transplantation. Unless you indicate otherwise, consent to make anatomical gifts may also be given by a relative of a deceased person. However, because relatives are often in shock or too upset to make such a decision, it is better to have one's intent made clear before death.

The easiest way for a person to express his or her consent to make anatomical gifts is by signing the back side of his or her New York state license stating that you are willing to be considered as an organ donor. Your signature must be made in the presence of two witnesses who must also sign their names.

Consent to make anatomical gifts can also be made in the will, and New York law provides that such gifts become effective immediately on death without the necessity of probating the will and even despite the invalidity of a will.

If a document or will has been delivered to a specified donee, it may be amended or revoked in the following ways:

☛ By executing and delivering a signed statement to the donee.

☛ By an oral statement of revocation made in the presence of two persons, communicated to the donee.

- By a statement made during a terminal illness to an attending physician and communicated to the donee.

- By a signed card or document found on the person of the donor or in his or her effects. A donor card is included in this book on page 105.

If any document of gift has not been delivered to a donee, it may be revoked by any of the above methods or by destruction, cancellation, or mutilation of the document and all executed copies of the document.

# APPENDIX A
# SAMPLE WILLS AND FORMS

The following pages include sample filled-in forms for some of the wills in this book. They are filled out in different ways for different situations. You should look at all of them to see how the different sections can be filled in. Only one example of a self-proved will affidavit is shown, but you should use it with every will.

# Last Will and Testament

I, ___John Smith_____ a resident of ___Tioga_____ County, New York do hereby make, publish, and declare this to be my Last Will and Testament, hereby revoking any and all Wills and Codicils heretofore made by me.

FIRST: I direct that all my just debts and funeral expenses be paid out of my estate as soon after my death as is practicable.

SECOND: I give, devise, and bequeath the following specific gifts:
_the gold watch which I got from my grandfather to my brother Ned Smith._____
----------------------------------------------------------------------
----------------------------------------------------------------------
----------------------------------------------------------------------

THIRD: I give, devise, and bequeath the rest, residue and remainder of my estate, real, personal, and mixed, of whatever kind and wherever situated, of which I may die seized or possessed, or in which I may have any interest or over which I may have any power of appointment or testamentary disposition, to my spouse, ___Barbara Smith_____. If my said spouse does not survive me, I give, devise and bequeath the said property to _my sisters, Jan Smith,_____ _Joan Smith, and Jennifer Smith in equal shares---------------------------- ------------------------------------------------------------------------,_ or the survivor of them.

FOURTH: In the event that any beneficiary fails to survive me by thirty days, then this will shall take effect as if that person had predeceased me.

FIFTH: I hereby nominate, constitute, and appoint ___Barbara Smith_____ as Executor/Executrix of this, my Last Will and Testament. In the event that such named person is unable or unwilling to serve at any time or for any reason, then I nominate, constitute, and appoint ___Reginald Smith_____ as Executor/Executrix in the place and stead of the person first named herein. It is my will and I direct that my Executor/Executrix shall not be required to furnish a bond for the faithful performance of his or her duties in any jurisdiction, any provision of law to the contrary notwithstanding, and I give my Executor/Executrix full power to administer my estate, including the power to settle claims, pay debts, and sell, lease or exchange real and personal property without court order.

IN WITNESS WHEREOF, I declare this to be my Last Will and Testament and execute it willingly as my free and voluntary act for the purposes expressed herein and I am of legal age and sound mind and make this under no constraint or undue influence, this _29th_ day of _January_____, 2002 at ___Oswego_____ State of ___New York_____.

_____ *John Smith* _____ L.S.

The foregoing instrument was on said date subscribed at the end thereof by _____ John Smith _____, the above named Testator who signed, published, and declared this instrument to be his/her Last Will and Testament in the presence of us and each of us, who thereupon at his/her request, in his/her presence, and in the presence of each other, have hereunto subscribed our names as witnesses thereto. We are of sound mind and proper age to witness a will and understand this to be his/her will, and to the best of our knowledge testator is of legal age to make a will, of sound mind, and under no constraint or undue influence.

_____ *Brenda Jones* _____ residing at _____ Oswego, New York _____

_____ *John Doe* _____ residing at _____ Ithaca, New York _____

# Last Will and Testament

I, _____John Smith_____ a resident of ___Tioga___ County, New York do hereby make, publish, and declare this to be my Last Will and Testament, hereby revoking any and all Wills and Codicils heretofore made by me.

FIRST: I direct that all my just debts and funeral expenses be paid out of my estate as soon after my death as is practicable.

SECOND:  I give, devise, and bequeath the following specific gifts:
10 shares of Applebee's stock to my aunt, Martha Brown ---------------------
------------------------------------------------------------------------------
------------------------------------------------------------------------------
------------------------------------------------------------------------------

THIRD: I give, devise, and bequeath the rest, residue and remainder of my estate, real, personal, and mixed, of whatever kind and wherever situated, of which I may die seized or possessed, or in which I may have any interest or over which I may have any power of appointment or testamentary disposition, to my spouse, _Barbara Smith_ _____--------------------_. If my said spouse does not survive me, I give, devise and bequeath the said property to my children _Amy Smith,_____ _Beamy Smith, and Seamy Smith---------------------------------------------_ _--------------------------------------------------------------------,_ in equal shares or to their lineal descendants, per stirpes.

FOURTH: In the event that any beneficiary fails to survive me by thirty days, then this will shall take effect as if that person had predeceased me.

FIFTH: I hereby nominate, constitute, and appoint ___Barbara Smith___ as Executor/Executrix of this, my Last Will and Testament. In the event that such named person is unable or unwilling to serve at any time or for any reason, then I nominate, constitute, and appoint ___Reginald Smith___ as Executor/Executrix in the place and stead of the person first named herein. It is my will and I direct that my Executor/Executrix shall not be required to furnish a bond for the faithful performance of his or her duties in any jurisdiction, any provision of law to the contrary notwithstanding, and I give my Executor/Executrix full power to administer my estate, including the power to settle claims, pay debts, and sell, lease or exchange real and personal property without court order.

IN WITNESS WHEREOF, I declare this to be my Last Will and Testament and execute it willingly as my free and voluntary act for the purposes expressed herein and I am of legal age and sound mind and make this under no constraint or undue influence, this _5th_ day of _January_____, 2002_ at _____Oswego_____ State of _____New York_____.

_____John Smith_____ L.S.

The foregoing instrument was on said date subscribed at the end thereof by _____John Smith_____, the above named Testator who signed, published, and declared this instrument to be his/her Last Will and Testament in the presence of us and each of us, who thereupon at his/her request, in his/her presence, and in the presence of each other, have hereunto subscribed our names as witnesses thereto. We are of sound mind and proper age to witness a will and understand this to be his/her will, and to the best of our knowledge testator is of legal age to make a will, of sound mind, and under no constraint or undue influence.

_____*Brenda Jones*_____ residing at___Oswego, New York_____

_____*John Doe*_____ residing at___Ithaca, New York_____

# Last Will and Testament

I, <u>Lester Doe</u> a resident of <u>Westchester</u> County, New York do hereby make, publish, and declare this to be my Last Will and Testament, hereby revoking any and all Wills and Codicils heretofore made by me.

FIRST: I direct that all my just debts and funeral expenses be paid out of my estate as soon after my death as is practicable.

SECOND: I give, devise, and bequeath the following specific gifts:
<u>None</u> -------------------------------------------------------------
--------------------------------------------------------------------
--------------------------------------------------------------------
--------------------------------------------------------------------

THIRD: I give, devise, and bequeath the rest, residue and remainder of my estate, real, personal, and mixed, of whatever kind and wherever situated, of which I may die seized or possessed, or in which I may have any interest or over which I may have any power of appointment or testamentary disposition, to my children <u>James Doe, Mary Doe,</u> <u>Larry Doe, Barry Doe, Carrie Doe, and Moe Doe</u> -------------------------
--------------------------------------------------------------------
--------------------------------------------------------------------
-----------------------------------------------------------, plus any afterborn or adopted children in equal shares or to their lineal descendants per stirpes.

FOURTH: In the event that any beneficiary fails to survive me by thirty days, then this will shall take effect as if that person had predeceased me.

FIFTH: In the event any of my children have not attained the age of 18 years at the time of my death, I hereby nominate, constitute, and appoint <u>Herbert Doe</u> <u></u> as guardian over the person of any of my children who have not reached the age of majority at the time of my death. In the event that said guardian is unable or unwilling to serve, then I nominate, constitute, and appoint <u>Tom Doe</u> <u></u> as guardian. Said guardian shall serve without bond or surety.

SIXTH: In the event any of my children have not attained the age of 18 years at the time of my death, I hereby nominate, constitute, and appoint <u>Joanna Doe</u> <u></u> as guardian over the estate of any of my children who have not reached the age of majority at the time of my death. In the event that said guardian is unable or unwilling to serve, then I nominate, constitute, and appoint <u>Missy Doe</u> <u></u> as guardian. Said guardian shall serve without bond or surety.

SEVENTH: I hereby nominate, constitute, and appoint ___Clarence Doe___ as Executor/Executrix of this, my Last Will and Testament. In the event that such named person is unable or unwilling to serve at any time or for any reason, then I nominate, constitute, and appoint ___Englebert Doe___ as Executor/Executrix in the place and stead of the person first named herein. It is my will and I direct that my Executor/Executrix shall not be required to furnish a bond for the faithful performance of his or her duties in any jurisdiction, any provision of law to the contrary notwithstanding, and I give my Executor/Executrix full power to administer my estate, including the power to settle claims, pay debts, and sell, lease or exchange real and personal property without court order.

IN WITNESS WHEREOF, I declare this to be my Last Will and Testament and execute it willingly as my free and voluntary act for the purposes expressed herein and I am of legal age and sound mind and make this under no constraint or undue influence, this _2nd_ day of _July_, _2003_ at _White Plains_ State of _New York_.

_____*John Doe*_____L.S.

The foregoing instrument was on said date subscribed at the end thereof by ___John Doe___, the above named Testator who signed, published, and declared this instrument to be his/her Last Will and Testament in the presence of us and each of us, who thereupon at his/her request, in his/her presence, and in the presence of each other, have hereunto subscribed our names as witnesses thereto. We are of sound mind and proper age to witness a will and understand this to be his/her will, and to the best of our knowledge testator is of legal age to make a will, of sound mind, and under no constraint or undue influence.

_*Jane Roe*_____residing at_White Plains, New York_____

_*Melvin Coe*_____residing at_Yonkers, New York_____

# Last Will and Testament

I, _____Mary Smith_____ a resident of ____Westchester_____ County, New York do hereby make, publish, and declare this to be my Last Will and Testament, hereby revoking any and all Wills and Codicils heretofore made by me.

FIRST: I direct that all my just debts and funeral expenses be paid out of my estate as soon after my death as is practicable.

SECOND: I give, devise, and bequeath the following specific gifts: my various kitchen utensils, including but not limited to, my 12-piece Baker's Secret pan set to my daughter, Janey Walters. ------------------------------ ------------------------------------------------------------------- -------------------------------------------------------------------

THIRD: I give, devise, and bequeath the rest, residue and remainder of my estate, real, personal, and mixed, of whatever kind and wherever situated, of which I may die seized or possessed, or in which I may have any interest or over which I may have any power of appointment or testamentary disposition, to the following: House in Vermont to grandson, Ralph Walters.------------------------------------------- ------------------------------------------------------------------- -------------------------------------------------------------------, or to the survivor of them.

FOURTH: In the event that any beneficiary fails to survive me by thirty days, then this will shall take effect as if that person had predeceased me.

FIFTH: I hereby nominate, constitute, and appoint __Regina Walters_____ as Executor/Executrix of this, my Last Will and Testament. In the event that such named person is unable or unwilling to serve at any time or for any reason, then I nominate, constitute, and appoint _____Tom Doe_____ as Executor/Executrix in the place and stead of the person first named herein. It is my will and I direct that my Executor/Executrix shall not be required to furnish a bond for the faithful performance of his or her duties in any jurisdiction, any provision of law to the contrary notwithstanding, and I give my Executor/Executrix full power to administer my estate, including the power to settle claims, pay debts, and sell, lease or exchange real and personal property without court order.

IN WITNESS WHEREOF, I declare this to be my Last Will and Testament and execute it willingly as my free and voluntary act for the purposes expressed herein and I am of legal age and sound mind and make this under no constraint or undue influence, this _6th_ day of _May_____, 2004 at ___White Plains___ State of __New York_____.

_____Mary Smith_____ L.S.

The foregoing instrument was on said date subscribed at the end thereof by
_____ Mary Smith _____, the above named Testator who signed, published, and declared this instrument to be his/her Last Will and Testament in the presence of us and each of us, who thereupon at his/her request, in his/her presence, and in the presence of each other, have hereunto subscribed our names as witnesses thereto. We are of sound mind and proper age to witness a will and understand this to be his/her will, and to the best of our knowledge testator is of legal age to make a will, of sound mind, and under no constraint or undue influence.

_____ Leon Brown _____ residing at_ New York City, New York _____

_____ Mildred Brown _____ residing at_ Huntington Station, New York ___

_____ Manuela Jacobs _____ residing at New York City, New York

(*Note:* Because the testator owns property in Vermont and that state requires three witnesses, an additional witness line has been added.)

# Self-Proved Will Affidavit

(attach to Will)

STATE OF NEW YORK

COUNTY OF __Westchester__

Each of the undersigned, individually and severally being duly sworn deposes and says:

The within will was subscribed in our presence and sight at the end thereof by ___John Doe___, the within named testat_or_, on the _5th_ day of ___July,___, _2003_, at ___three___ o'clock.

Said testat_or_ at the time of making such subscription declared the instrument so subscribed to be h_is_ last will.

Each of the undersigned thereupon signed h_er/his_ name as a witness at the end of said will at the request of said testat_or_ and in h_is_ presence and sight and in the presence and sight of each other.

Said testat_or_ was, at the time of so executing said will, over the age of 18 years and, in the respective opinions of the undersigned, of sound mind, memory and understanding and not under any restraint or in any respect incompetent to make a will.

The testat_or_, in the respective opinions of the undersigned, could read, write and converse in the English language and was suffering from no defect of sight, hearing or speech, or from any other physical or mental impairment which would affect h_is_ capacity to make a valid will. The will was executed as a single, original instrument and was not executed in counterparts.

Each of the undersigned was acquainted with said testat_or_ at such time and makes this affidavit at h_is_ request.

The within will was shown to the undersigned at the time this affidavit was made, and was examined by each of them as to the signature of said testat_____ and of the undersigned.

_Jane Roe_____ (Witness)

_Melvin Coe_____ (Witness)

Subscribed, sworn and acknowledged before me by ___John Doe_____, the testator, and by ___Melvin Coe_____ and ___Jane Roe_____ _____, witnesses, this _5th_ day of ___July, 2003_____.

___C.U. Sine_____
Notary or other officer

# Codicil to the Will of

Larry Lowe

I, _____ Larry Lowe _____, a resident of _____ Leon _____ County, New York declare this to be the first codicil to my Last Will and Testament dated _____ July 5 _____, __ 2001 __.

FIRST: I hereby revoke the clause of my Will which reads as follows:
FOURTH: I hereby leave $5000.00 to my daughter Mildred ---------------------
-----------------------------------------------------------------------------
-----------------------------------------------------------------------------
-----------------------------------------------------------------------------.

SECOND: I hereby add the following clause to my Will: _____
FOURTH: I hereby leave $1000.00 to my daughter Mildred ---------------------
-----------------------------------------------------------------------------
-----------------------------------------------------------------------------
-----------------------------------------------------------------------------.

THIRD: In all other respects I hereby confirm and republish my Last Will and Testament dated _____ July 5 _____, ___ 2001 ___.

IN WITNESS WHEREOF, I have signed, published, and declared the foregoing instrument as and for a codicil to my Last Will and Testament, this ___ 5th ___ day of _____ January _____, __ 2002 __.

*Larry Lowe*
_____

The foregoing instrument was on the _5th_ day of _____ January _____, __ 2002 __, signed at the end thereof, and at the same time published and declared by _____ Larry Lowe _____, as and for a codicil to his/her Last Will and Testament, dated _____ July 5 _____, ___ 2001 ___, in the presence of each of us, who, this attestation clause having been read to us, did at the request of the said testator/testatrix, in his/her presence and in the presence of each other signed our names as witnesses thereto.

*James Smith*
_____residing at___ Binghamton, New York ___

*Mary Smith*
_____residing at___ Elmira, New York ___

# Living Will

Declaration made this __29__ day of __January__ , __2002__ . I, __Norman Milquetoast__ , willfully and voluntarily make known my desire that my dying not be artificially prolonged under the circumstances set forth below, and I do hereby declare:

If at any time I have a terminal condition and if my attending or treating physician and another consulting physician have determined that there can be no medical probability of my recovery from such condition, I direct that life-prolonging procedures be withheld or withdrawn when the application of such procedures would serve only to prolong artificially the process of dying, and that I be permitted to die naturally with only the administration of medication or the performance of any medical procedure deemed necessary to provide me with comfort, care or alleviate pain.

It is my intention that this declaration be honored by my family and physician as the final expression of my legal right to refuse medical or surgical treatment and to accept the consequences for such refusal.

This authorization includes ( x ) does not include (  ) the withholding or withdrawal of artificial feeding and hydration (check only one box above).

Special Instructions (if any) _____ None. ----------------------------------

-------------------------------------------------------------------------

-------------------------------------------------------------------------

-------------------------------------------------------------------------

Signed this __29th__ day of __January__ , __2002__ .

*Norman Milquetoast*
Signature
Address: __1234 New York Avenue__
__South Nyack, NY 10961__

I understand the full import of this declaration, and am emotionally and mentally competent to make this declaration.

Additional instructions (optional):

None ------------------------------------------------------------------

-------------------------------------------------------------------------

*Norman Milquetoast*
(Signed)

*Harvey Nabor*
Witness
__1236 New York Avenue__
__South Nyack, NY 10961__
Address
__914-555-2121__
Phone

*June Nabor*
Witness
__1236 New York Avenue__
__South Nyack, NY 10961__
Address
__914-555-2121__
Phone

# APPENDIX B
# WILLS AND FORMS

The following pages contain forms that can be used to prepare a will, codicil, living will, and Uniform Donor Card. They should only be used by persons who have read this book, who do not have any complications in their legal affairs and who understand the forms they are using. The forms may be used right out of the book or they may be photocopied or retyped. Two copies of each form are included.

**Form 1. Asset and Beneficiary List**—*Use this form to keep an accurate record of your estate as well as your beneficiaries' names and addresses.*

**Form 2. Preferences and Information List**—*Use this form to let your family know of your wishes on matters not usually included in a will.*

**Form 3. Simple Will**—Spouse and Minor Children—One Guardian. *Use this will if you have minor children and want all your property to go to your spouse, but if your spouse dies previously, then to your minor children. It provides for one person to be guardian over your children and their estates.*

**Form 4. Simple Will**—Spouse and Minor Children—Two Guardians. *Use this will if you have minor children and want all your property to go to your spouse, but if your spouse dies previously, then to your minor children. It provides for two guardians, one over your children and one over their estates.*

**Form 5. Simple Will**—Spouse and Minor Children—Guardian and Trust. *This will should be used if you have minor children and want all your property to go to your spouse, but if your spouse dies previously, then to your minor children. It provides for one person to be guardian over your* *children and for either the same person or another to be trustee over their property. This will allows your children's property to be held until they are older than eighteen rather than distributing it all to them at age eighteen.*

**Form 6. Simple Will**—Spouse and No Children. *Use this will if you want your property to go to your spouse but if your spouse predeceases you, to others or the **survivor** of the others.*

**Form 7. Simple Will**—Spouse and No Children. *Use this will if you want your property to go to your spouse but if your spouse predeceases you, to others or the **descendants** of the others.*

**Form 8. Simple Will**—Spouse and Adult Children. *Use this will if you want all of your property to go to your spouse, but if your spouse dies previously, then to your children, all of whom are adults.*

**Form 9. Simple Will**—Spouse and Adult Children. *Use this will if you want some of your property to go to your spouse, and some of your property to your children, all of whom are adults.*

**Form 10. Simple Will**—No Spouse—Minor Children—One Guardian. *Use this will if you do not have a spouse and want all your property to go to your children, at least one of whom is a minor. It provides for one person to be guardian over your children and their estates.*

**Form 11. Simple Will**—No Spouse—Minor Children—Two Guardians. *Use this will if you do not have a spouse and want all your property to go to your children, at least one of whom is a minor. It provides for two guardians, one over your children and one over their estates.*

**Form 12. Simple Will**—No Spouse—Minor Children—Guardian and Trust. *Use this will if you do not have a spouse and want all your property to go to your children, at least one of whom is a minor. It provides for one person to be guardian over your children and for either that person or another to be trustee over their property. This will allows your children's property to be held until they are older than eighteen rather than distributing it all to them at age eighteen.*

**Form 13. Simple Will**—No Spouse—Adult Children. *This will should be used if you wish to leave your property to your adult children, or equally to each **family** if they predecease you.*

**Form 14. Simple Will**—No Spouse—Adult Children. *This will should be used if you wish to leave your property to your adult children, or equally to each **person** if they predecease you.*

**Form 15. Simple Will**—No Spouse and No Children. *Use this will if you have no spouse or children and want your property to go to the **survivor** of the people you name.*

**Form 16. Simple Will**—No Spouse and No Children. *Use this will if you have no spouse or children and want your property to go to the **descendants** of the people you name.*

**Form 17. Self-Proved Will Page**. *This page should be attached to every will as the last page. It must be witnessed and notarized.*

**Form 18. Codicil to Will**. *This form can be used to change one section of your will. Usually it is just as easy to execute a new will, since all of the same formalities are required.*

**Form 19. Self-Proved Codicil Page**. *If you decided to execute a codicil instead of making a new will, this page should be attached to your codicil as the last page. It must be witnessed and notarized.*

**Form 20. Living Will**. *This is a document which expresses your desire to withhold certain extraordinary medical treatment should you have a terminal illness and you reach such a state that your wishes to withhold such treatment cannot be determined.*

**Form 21. Organ Donor Card**. *This form is used to spell out your wishes for donation of your body or any organs.*

# HOW TO PICK THE RIGHT WILL

Follow the chart and use the form number in the black circle,
then use Form 17, the self-proving affidavit.

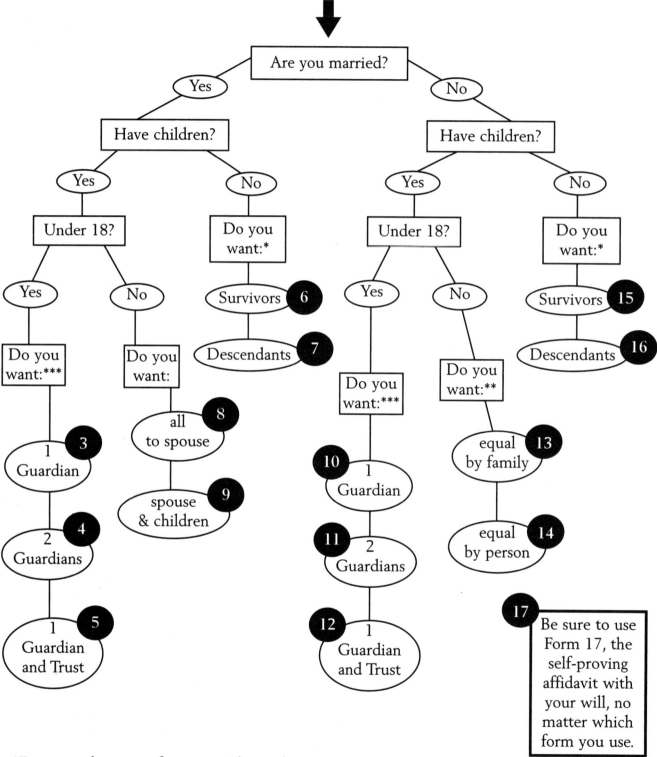

*For an explanation of survivors/descendants, see page 27.

**For an explanation of families/persons, see page 28.

*** For an explanation of children's guardians and trust, see pages 30-31

# Asset and Beneficiary List

Property Inventory

**Assets**

Bank Accounts (checking, savings, certificates of deposit)

_____
_____
_____
_____
_____
_____
_____

Real Estate

_____
_____
_____
_____
_____
_____
_____
_____

Vehicles (cars, trucks, boats, planes, RVs, etc.)

_____
_____
_____
_____
_____
_____
_____

Personal Property (collections, jewelry, tools, artwork, household items, etc.)

_____
_____
_____
_____
_____
_____

_____
_____
_____
_____
_____
_____
_____
_____

## Stocks/Bonds/Mutual Funds

_____
_____
_____
_____
_____
_____
_____
_____
_____
_____
_____
_____
_____
_____
_____

## Retirement Accounts (IRAs, 401(k)s, pension plans, etc.)

_____
_____
_____
_____
_____
_____
_____

## Receivables (mortgages held, notes, accounts receivable, personal loans)

_____
_____
_____
_____
_____
_____

Life Insurance

_____
_____
_____
_____
_____
_____
_____

Other Property (trusts, partnerships, businesses, profit sharing, copyrights, etc.)

_____
_____
_____
_____
_____
_____
_____

## Liabilities

Real Estate Loans

_____
_____
_____
_____
_____
_____

Vehicle Loans

_____
_____
_____
_____
_____
_____

Other Secured Loans

_____
_____
_____
_____
_____
_____
_____
_____

Unsecured Loans and Debts (taxes, child support, judgments, etc.)

_____
_____
_____
_____
_____
_____
_____
_____

**Beneficiary List**

Name_____ Address_____ Phone_____

_____
_____
_____
_____
_____
_____
_____
_____

# Preferences and Information List

## STATEMENT OF DESIRES AND LOCATION OF PROPERTY & DOCUMENTS

I, _____, am signing this document as the expression of my desires as to the matters stated below, and to inform my family members or other significant persons of the location of certain property and documents in the event of any emergency or of my death.

1.  **Funeral Desires.** It is my desire that the following arrangements be made for my funeral and disposition of remains in the event of my death (state if you have made any arrangements, such as pre-paid burial plans, cemetery plots owned, etc.):

    ❏  Burial at _____
    _____.

    ❏  Cremation at _____
    _____.

    ❏  Other specific desires: _____
    _____
    _____.

2.  **Pets.** I have the following pet(s): _____
    _____. The following are my desires concerning the
    care of said pet(s): _____
    _____
    _____.

4.  **Notification.** I would like the following person(s) notified in the event of emergency or death (give name, address and phone number):

    _____
    _____
    _____
    _____
    _____
    _____.

5.  **Location of Documents.** The following is a list of important documents, and their location:

    ❏  Last Will and Testament, dated _____. Location: _____
    _____.

    ❏  Durable Power of Attorney, dated _____. Location: _____
    _____.

    ❏  Living Will, dated _____. Location: _____
    _____.

    ❏  Deed(s) to real estate (describe property location and location of deed):
    _____
    _____
    _____

❏ Title(s) to vehicles (cars, boats, etc.) (Describe vehicle, its location, and location of title, registration, or other documents):

_____
_____
_____
_____

❏ Life insurance policies (list name address & phone number of insurance company and insurance agent, policy number, and location of policy):

_____
_____
_____

❏ Other insurance policies (list type, company & agent, policy number, and location of policy):

_____
_____
_____

❏ Other: (list other documents such as stock certificates, bonds, certificates of deposit, etc., and their location):

_____
_____
_____

6. **Location of Assets.** In addition to items readily visible in my home or listed above, I have the following assets:

❏ Safe deposit box located at _____, box number _____. Key located at: _____.

❏ Bank accounts (list name & address of bank, type of account, and account number):

_____

❏ Other (describe the item and give its location):

_____
_____
_____
_____
_____

7. Other desires or information (state any desires or provide any information not given above; use additional sheets of paper if necessary):

_____
_____
_____
_____
_____

Dated: _____

_____
Signature

# Last Will and Testament

I, _____ a resident of _____ County, New York do hereby make, publish, and declare this to be my Last Will and Testament, hereby revoking any and all Wills and Codicils heretofore made by me.

FIRST: I direct that all my just debts and funeral expenses be paid out of my estate as soon after my death as is practicable.

SECOND: I give, devise, and bequeath the following specific gifts:

_____
_____
_____

THIRD: I give, devise, and bequeath the rest, residue and remainder of my estate, real, personal, and mixed, of whatever kind and wherever situated, of which I may die seized or possessed, or in which I may have any interest or over which I may have any power of appointment or testamentary disposition, to my spouse, _____ _____. If my said spouse does not survive me, I give, devise and bequeath the said property to my children_____ _____ _____, plus any afterborn or adopted children in equal shares or their lineal descendants, per stirpes.

FOURTH: In the event that any beneficiary fails to survive me by thirty days, then this will shall take effect as if that person had predeceased me.

FIFTH: Should my spouse not survive me, I hereby nominate, constitute, and appoint _____ as guardian over the person and estate of any of my children who have not reached the age of majority at the time of my death. In the event that said guardian is unable or unwilling to serve, then I nominate, constitute, and appoint _____ as guardian. Said guardian shall serve without bond or surety.

SIXTH: I hereby nominate, constitute, and appoint _____ _____ as Executor/Executrix of this, my Last Will and Testament. In the event that such named person is unable or unwilling to serve at any time or for any reason, then I nominate, constitute, and appoint _____ as Executor/Executrix in the place and stead of the person first named herein. It is my will and I direct that my Executor/Executrix shall not be required to furnish a bond for the faithful performance of his or her duties in any jurisdiction, any provision of law to the contrary notwithstanding, and I give my Executor/Executrix full power to administer my estate, including the power to settle claims, pay debts, and sell, lease or exchange real and personal property without court order.

IN WITNESS WHEREOF, I declare this to be my Last Will and Testament and execute it willingly as my free and voluntary act for the purposes expressed herein and I am of legal age and sound mind and make this under no constraint or undue influence, this _____ day of _____, _____ at _____ State of _____.

_____L.S.

The foregoing instrument was on said date subscribed at the end thereof by _____, the above named Testator who signed, published, and declared this instrument to be his/her Last Will and Testament in the presence of us and each of us, who thereupon at his/her request, in his/her presence, and in the presence of each other, have hereunto subscribed our names as witnesses thereto. We are of sound mind and proper age to witness a will and understand this to be his/her will, and to the best of our knowledge testator is of legal age to make a will, of sound mind, and under no constraint or undue influence.

_____residing at_____

_____residing at_____

# Last Will and Testament

I, _____ a resident of _____ County, New York do hereby make, publish, and declare this to be my Last Will and Testament, hereby revoking any and all Wills and Codicils heretofore made by me.

FIRST: I direct that all my just debts and funeral expenses be paid out of my estate as soon after my death as is practicable.

SECOND: I give, devise, and bequeath the following specific gifts:

_____

_____

_____

_____

THIRD: I give, devise, and bequeath the rest, residue and remainder of my estate, real, personal, and mixed, of whatever kind and wherever situated, of which I may die seized or possessed, or in which I may have any interest or over which I may have any power of appointment or testamentary disposition, to my spouse, _____ _____. If my said spouse does not survive me, I give, devise and bequeath the said property to my children _____ _____ _____, plus any afterborn or adopted children in equal shares or their lineal descendants, per stirpes.

FOURTH: In the event that any beneficiary fails to survive me by thirty days, then this will shall take effect as if that person had predeceased me.

FIFTH: Should my spouse not survive me, I hereby nominate, constitute, and appoint _____, as guardian over the person of any of my children who have not reached the age of majority at the time of my death. In the event that said guardian is unable or unwilling to serve, then I nominate, constitute, and appoint _____ _____ as guardian. Said guardian shall serve without bond or surety.

SIXTH: Should my spouse not survive me, I hereby nominate, constitute, and appoint _____ as guardian over the estate of any of my children who have not reached the age of majority at the time of my death. In the event that said guardian is unable or unwilling to serve, then I nominate, constitute, and appoint _____ _____ as guardian. Said guardian shall serve without bond or surety.

SEVENTH: I hereby nominate, constitute, and appoint _____ _____ as Executor/Executrix of this, my Last Will and Testament. In the event that such named person is unable or unwilling to serve at any time or for any reason, then I nominate, constitute, and appoint _____ as Executor/Executrix in the place and stead of the person first named herein. It is my will and I direct that my Executor/Executrix shall not be required to furnish a bond for the faithful performance of his or her duties in any jurisdiction, any provision of law to the contrary notwithstanding, and I give my Executor/Executrix full power to administer my estate, including the power to settle claims, pay debts, and sell, lease or exchange real and personal property without court order.

IN WITNESS WHEREOF, I declare this to be my Last Will and Testament and execute it willingly as my free and voluntary act for the purposes expressed herein and I am of legal age and sound mind and make this under no constraint or undue influence, this _____ day of _____, _____ at _____ State of _____.

_____L.S.

The foregoing instrument was on said date subscribed at the end thereof by _____, the above named Testator who signed, published, and declared this instrument to be his/her Last Will and Testament in the presence of us and each of us, who thereupon at his/her request, in his/her presence, and in the presence of each other, have hereunto subscribed our names as witnesses thereto. We are of sound mind and proper age to witness a will and understand this to be his/her will, and to the best of our knowledge testator is of legal age to make a will, of sound mind, and under no constraint or undue influence.

_____residing at_____

_____residing at_____

# Last Will and Testament

I, _____ a resident of _____ County, New York do hereby make, publish, and declare this to be my Last Will and Testament, hereby revoking any and all Wills and Codicils heretofore made by me.

FIRST: I direct that all my just debts and funeral expenses be paid out of my estate as soon after my death as is practicable.

SECOND: I give, devise, and bequeath the following specific gifts:

_____

_____

_____

THIRD: I give, devise, and bequeath the rest, residue and remainder of my estate, real, personal, and mixed, of whatever kind and wherever situated, of which I may die seized or possessed, or in which I may have any interest or over which I may have any power of appointment or testamentary disposition, to my spouse, _____. If my said spouse does not survive me, I give, devise and bequeath the said property to my children _____

_____

_____,

plus any afterborn or adopted children in equal shares or their lineal descendants, per stirpes.

FOURTH: In the event that any beneficiary fails to survive me by thirty days, then this will shall take effect as if that person had predeceased me.

FIFTH: In the event that any of my children have not reached the age of _____ years at the time of my death, then the share of any such child shall be held in a separate trust by _____ for such child.

The trustee shall use the income and that part of the principal of the trust as is, in the trustee's sole discretion, necessary or desirable to provide proper housing, medical care, food, clothing, entertainment and education for the trust beneficiary, considering the beneficiary's other resources. Any income that is not distributed shall be added to the principal. Additionally, the trustee shall have all powers conferred by the law of the state having jurisdiction over this trust, as well as the power to pay from the assets of the trust reasonable fees necessary to administer the trust.

The trust shall terminate when the child reaches the age specified above and the remaining assets distributed to the child, unless they have been exhausted sooner. In the event the child dies prior to the termination of the trust, then the assets shall pass to the estate of the child. The interests of the beneficiary under this trust shall not be assignable and shall be free from the claims of creditors to the full extent allowed by law.

In the event the said trustee is unable or unwilling to serve for any reason, then I nominate, constitute, and appoint _____ as alternate trustee. No bond shall be required of either trustee in any jurisdiction and this trust shall be administered without court supervision as allowed by law.

SIXTH: Should my spouse not survive me, I hereby nominate, constitute, and appoint _____ as guardian over the person and estate of any of my children who have not reached the age of majority at the time of my death. In the event that said guardian is unable or unwilling to serve, then I nominate, constitute, and appoint _____ as guardian.

SEVENTH: I hereby nominate, constitute, and appoint _____ as Executor/Executrix of this, my Last Will and Testament. In the event that such named person is unable or unwilling to serve at any time or for any reason, then I nominate, constitute, and appoint _____ as Executor/Executrix in the place and stead of the person first named herein. It is my will and I direct that my Executor/Executrix shall not be required to furnish a bond for the faithful performance of his or her duties in any jurisdiction, any provision of law to the contrary notwithstanding, and I give my Executor/Executrix full power to administer my estate, including the power to settle claims, pay debts, and sell, lease or exchange real and personal property without court order.

IN WITNESS WHEREOF, I declare this to be my Last Will and Testament and execute it willingly as my free and voluntary act for the purposes expressed herein and I am of legal age and sound mind and make this under no constraint or undue influence, this _____ day of _____, _____ at _____ State of _____.

_____L.S.

The foregoing instrument was on said date subscribed at the end thereof by _____, the above named Testator who signed, published, and declared this instrument to be his/her Last Will and Testament in the presence of us and each of us, who thereupon at his/her request, in his/her presence, and in the presence of each other, have hereunto subscribed our names as witnesses thereto. We are of sound mind and proper age to witness a will and understand this to be his/her will, and to the best of our knowledge testator is of legal age to make a will, of sound mind, and under no constraint or undue influence.

_____residing at_____

_____residing at_____

# Last Will and Testament

I, _____ a resident of _____ County, New York do hereby make, publish, and declare this to be my Last Will and Testament, hereby revoking any and all Wills and Codicils heretofore made by me.

FIRST: I direct that all my just debts and funeral expenses be paid out of my estate as soon after my death as is practicable.

SECOND: I give, devise, and bequeath the following specific gifts:

_____

_____

_____

THIRD: I give, devise, and bequeath the rest, residue and remainder of my estate, real, personal, and mixed, of whatever kind and wherever situated, of which I may die seized or possessed, or in which I may have any interest or over which I may have any power of appointment or testamentary disposition, to my spouse, _____ _____. If my said spouse does not survive me, I give, devise and bequeath the said property to _____

_____

_____,

or the survivor of them.

FOURTH: In the event that any beneficiary fails to survive me by thirty days, then this will shall take effect as if that person had predeceased me.

FIFTH: I hereby nominate, constitute, and appoint _____ as Executor/Executrix of this, my Last Will and Testament. In the event that such named person is unable or unwilling to serve at any time or for any reason, then I nominate, constitute, and appoint _____ as Executor/Executrix in the place and stead of the person first named herein. It is my will and I direct that my Executor/Executrix shall not be required to furnish a bond for the faithful performance of his or her duties in any jurisdiction, any provision of law to the contrary notwithstanding, and I give my Executor/Executrix full power to administer my estate, including the power to settle claims, pay debts, and sell, lease or exchange real and personal property without court order.

IN WITNESS WHEREOF, I declare this to be my Last Will and Testament and execute it willingly as my free and voluntary act for the purposes expressed herein and I am of legal age and sound mind and make this under no constraint or undue influence, this _____ day of _____, _____ at _____ State of _____.

_____L.S.

The foregoing instrument was on said date subscribed at the end thereof by
_____, the above named Testator who signed, published, and declared this instrument to be his/her Last Will and Testament in the presence of us and each of us, who thereupon at his/her request, in his/her presence, and in the presence of each other, have hereunto subscribed our names as witnesses thereto. We are of sound mind and proper age to witness a will and understand this to be his/her will, and to the best of our knowledge testator is of legal age to make a will, of sound mind, and under no constraint or undue influence.

_____residing at_____

_____residing at_____

# Last Will and Testament

I, _____ a resident of _____ County, New York do hereby make, publish, and declare this to be my Last Will and Testament, hereby revoking any and all Wills and Codicils heretofore made by me.

FIRST: I direct that all my just debts and funeral expenses be paid out of my estate as soon after my death as is practicable.

SECOND: I give, devise, and bequeath the following specific gifts:

_____

_____

_____

THIRD: I give, devise, and bequeath the rest, residue and remainder of my estate, real, personal, and mixed, of whatever kind and wherever situated, of which I may die seized or possessed, or in which I may have any interest or over which I may have any power of appointment or testamentary disposition, to my spouse, _____ _____. If my said spouse does not survive me, I give, devise and bequeath the said property to_____ _____, _____, or to their lineal descendants, per stirpes.

FOURTH: In the event that any beneficiary fails to survive me by thirty days, then this will shall take effect as if that person had predeceased me.

FIFTH: I hereby nominate, constitute, and appoint _____ as Executor/Executrix of this, my Last Will and Testament. In the event that such named person is unable or unwilling to serve at any time or for any reason, then I nominate, constitute, and appoint _____ as Executor/Executrix in the place and stead of the person first named herein. It is my will and I direct that my Executor/Executrix shall not be required to furnish a bond for the faithful performance of his or her duties in any jurisdiction, any provision of law to the contrary notwithstanding, and I give my Executor/Executrix full power to administer my estate, including the power to settle claims, pay debts, and sell, lease or exchange real and personal property without court order.

IN WITNESS WHEREOF, I declare this to be my Last Will and Testament and execute it willingly as my free and voluntary act for the purposes expressed herein and I am of legal age and sound mind and make this under no constraint or undue influence, this _____ day of _____, _____ at _____ State of _____.

_____L.S.

The foregoing instrument was on said date subscribed at the end thereof by _____, the above named Testator who signed, published, and declared this instrument to be his/her Last Will and Testament in the presence of us and each of us, who thereupon at his/her request, in his/her presence, and in the presence of each other, have hereunto subscribed our names as witnesses thereto. We are of sound mind and proper age to witness a will and understand this to be his/her will, and to the best of our knowledge testator is of legal age to make a will, of sound mind, and under no constraint or undue influence.

_____residing at_____

_____residing at_____

# Last Will and Testament

I, _____ a resident of _____ County, New York do hereby make, publish, and declare this to be my Last Will and Testament, hereby revoking any and all Wills and Codicils heretofore made by me.

FIRST: I direct that all my just debts and funeral expenses be paid out of my estate as soon after my death as is practicable.

SECOND: I give, devise, and bequeath the following specific gifts:

_____

_____

_____

THIRD: I give, devise, and bequeath the rest, residue and remainder of my estate, real, personal, and mixed, of whatever kind and wherever situated, of which I may die seized or possessed, or in which I may have any interest or over which I may have any power of appointment or testamentary disposition, to my spouse, _____ _____. If my said spouse does not survive me, I give, devise and bequeath the said property to my children _____

_____

_____,

in equal shares or to their lineal descendants, per stirpes.

FOURTH: In the event that any beneficiary fails to survive me by thirty days, then this will shall take effect as if that person had predeceased me.

FIFTH: I hereby nominate, constitute, and appoint _____ as Executor/Executrix of this, my Last Will and Testament. In the event that such named person is unable or unwilling to serve at any time or for any reason, then I nominate, constitute, and appoint _____ as Executor/Executrix in the place and stead of the person first named herein. It is my will and I direct that my Executor/Executrix shall not be required to furnish a bond for the faithful performance of his or her duties in any jurisdiction, any provision of law to the contrary notwithstanding, and I give my Executor/Executrix full power to administer my estate, including the power to settle claims, pay debts, and sell, lease or exchange real and personal property without court order.

IN WITNESS WHEREOF, I declare this to be my Last Will and Testament and execute it willingly as my free and voluntary act for the purposes expressed herein and I am of legal age and sound mind and make this under no constraint or undue influence, this _____ day of _____, _____ at _____ State of _____.

_____L.S.

The foregoing instrument was on said date subscribed at the end thereof by
_____, the above named Testator who signed, published, and declared this instrument to be his/her Last Will and Testament in the presence of us and each of us, who thereupon at his/her request, in his/her presence, and in the presence of each other, have hereunto subscribed our names as witnesses thereto. We are of sound mind and proper age to witness a will and understand this to be his/her will, and to the best of our knowledge testator is of legal age to make a will, of sound mind, and under no constraint or undue influence.

_____residing at_____

_____residing at_____

# Last Will and Testament

I, _____ a resident of _____ County, New York do hereby make, publish, and declare this to be my Last Will and Testament, hereby revoking any and all Wills and Codicils heretofore made by me.

FIRST: I direct that all my just debts and funeral expenses be paid out of my estate as soon after my death as is practicable.

SECOND:  I give, devise, and bequeath the following specific gifts:

_____

_____

_____

THIRD: I give, devise, and bequeath the rest, residue and remainder of my estate, real, personal, and mixed, of whatever kind and wherever situated, of which I may die seized or possessed, or in which I may have any interest or over which I may have any power of appointment or testamentary disposition, as follows:

_____% to my spouse, _____ and

_____% to my children, _____

_____

_____,

in equal shares or to their lineal descendants per stirpes.

FOURTH: In the event that any beneficiary fails to survive me by thirty days, then this will shall take effect as if that person had predeceased me.

FIFTH: I hereby nominate, constitute, and appoint _____ as Executor/Executrix of this, my Last Will and Testament. In the event that such named person is unable or unwilling to serve at any time or for any reason, then I nominate, constitute, and appoint _____ as Executor/Executrix in the place and stead of the person first named herein. It is my will and I direct that my Executor/Executrix shall not be required to furnish a bond for the faithful performance of his or her duties in any jurisdiction, any provision of law to the contrary notwithstanding, and I give my Executor/Executrix full power to administer my estate, including the power to settle claims, pay debts, and sell, lease or exchange real and personal property without court order.

IN WITNESS WHEREOF, I declare this to be my Last Will and Testament and execute it willingly as my free and voluntary act for the purposes expressed herein and I am of legal age and sound mind and make this under no constraint or undue influence, this \_\_\_\_\_ day of _____, \_\_\_\_\_ at _____ State of _____.

_____L.S.

The foregoing instrument was on said date subscribed at the end thereof by _____, the above named Testator who signed, published, and declared this instrument to be his/her Last Will and Testament in the presence of us and each of us, who thereupon at his/her request, in his/her presence, and in the presence of each other, have hereunto subscribed our names as witnesses thereto. We are of sound mind and proper age to witness a will and understand this to be his/her will, and to the best of our knowledge testator is of legal age to make a will, of sound mind, and under no constraint or undue influence.

_____residing at_____

_____residing at_____

# Last Will and Testament

I, _____ a resident of _____ County, New York do hereby make, publish, and declare this to be my Last Will and Testament, hereby revoking any and all Wills and Codicils heretofore made by me.

FIRST: I direct that all my just debts and funeral expenses be paid out of my estate as soon after my death as is practicable.

SECOND: I give, devise, and bequeath the following specific gifts:

_____

_____

_____

THIRD: I give, devise, and bequeath the rest, residue and remainder of my estate, real, personal, and mixed, of whatever kind and wherever situated, of which I may die seized or possessed, or in which I may have any interest or over which I may have any power of appointment or testamentary disposition, to my children _____

_____

_____

_____  _____, plus any afterborn or adopted children in equal shares or to their lineal descendants per stirpes.

FOURTH: In the event that any beneficiary fails to survive me by thirty days, then this will shall take effect as if that person had predeceased me.

FIFTH: In the event any of my children have not attained the age of 18 years at the time of my death, I hereby nominate, constitute, and appoint _____ _____ as guardian over the person and estate of any of my children who have not reached the age of majority at the time of my death. In the event that said guardian is unable or unwilling to serve, then I nominate, constitute, and appoint _____ _____ as guardian. Said guardian shall serve without bond or surety.

SIXTH: I hereby nominate, constitute, and appoint _____ _____ as Executor/Executrix of this, my Last Will and Testament. In the event that such named person is unable or unwilling to serve at any time or for any reason, then I nominate, constitute, and appoint _____  _____ as Executor/Executrix in the place and stead of the person first named herein. It is my will and I direct that my Executor/Executrix shall not be required to furnish a bond for the faithful performance of his or her duties in any jurisdiction, any provision of law to the contrary notwithstanding, and I give my Executor/Executrix full power to administer my estate, including the power to settle claims, pay debts, and sell, lease or exchange real and personal property without court order.

IN WITNESS WHEREOF, I declare this to be my Last Will and Testament and execute it willingly as my free and voluntary act for the purposes expressed herein and I am of legal age and sound mind and make this under no constraint or undue influence, this _____ day of _____, _____ at _____ State of _____.

_____L.S.

The foregoing instrument was on said date subscribed at the end thereof by _____, the above named Testator who signed, published, and declared this instrument to be his/her Last Will and Testament in the presence of us and each of us, who thereupon at his/her request, in his/her presence, and in the presence of each other, have hereunto subscribed our names as witnesses thereto. We are of sound mind and proper age to witness a will and understand this to be his/her will, and to the best of our knowledge testator is of legal age to make a will, of sound mind, and under no constraint or undue influence.

_____residing at_____

_____residing at_____

# Last Will and Testament

I, _____ a resident of _____ County, New York do hereby make, publish, and declare this to be my Last Will and Testament, hereby revoking any and all Wills and Codicils heretofore made by me.

FIRST: I direct that all my just debts and funeral expenses be paid out of my estate as soon after my death as is practicable.

SECOND:  I give, devise, and bequeath the following specific gifts:

_____

_____

_____

THIRD: I give, devise, and bequeath the rest, residue and remainder my estate, real, personal, and mixed, of whatever kind and wherever situated, of which I may die seized or possessed, or in which I may have any interest or over which I may have any power of appointment or testamentary disposition, to my children _____

_____

_____

_____, plus any afterborn or adopted children in equal shares or to their lineal descendants per stirpes.

FOURTH: In the event that any beneficiary fails to survive me by thirty days, then this will shall take effect as if that person had predeceased me.

FIFTH: In the event any of my children have not attained the age of 18 years at the time of my death, I hereby nominate, constitute, and appoint _____ _____ as guardian over the person of any of my children who have not reached the age of majority at the time of my death. In the event that said guardian is unable or unwilling to serve, then I nominate, constitute, and appoint _____ _____ as guardian. Said guardian shall serve without bond or surety.

SIXTH: In the event any of my children have not attained the age of 18 years at the time of my death, I hereby nominate, constitute, and appoint _____ _____ as guardian over the estate of any of my children who have not reached the age of majority at the time of my death. In the event that said guardian is unable or unwilling to serve, then I nominate, constitute, and appoint _____ _____ as guardian. Said guardian shall serve without bond or surety.

SEVENTH: I hereby nominate, constitute, and appoint _____ as Executor/Executrix of this, my Last Will and Testament. In the event that such named person is unable or unwilling to serve at any time or for any reason, then I nominate, constitute, and appoint _____ as Executor/Executrix in the place and stead of the person first named herein. It is my will and I direct that my Executor/Executrix shall not be required to furnish a bond for the faithful performance of his or her duties in any jurisdiction, any provision of law to the contrary notwithstanding, and I give my Executor/Executrix full power to administer my estate, including the power to settle claims, pay debts, and sell, lease or exchange real and personal property without court order.

IN WITNESS WHEREOF, I declare this to be my Last Will and Testament and execute it willingly as my free and voluntary act for the purposes expressed herein and I am of legal age and sound mind and make this under no constraint or undue influence, this _____ day of _____, _____ at _____ State of _____.

_____L.S.


The foregoing instrument was on said date subscribed at the end thereof by _____, the above named Testator who signed, published, and declared this instrument to be his/her Last Will and Testament in the presence of us and each of us, who thereupon at his/her request, in his/her presence, and in the presence of each other, have hereunto subscribed our names as witnesses thereto. We are of sound mind and proper age to witness a will and understand this to be his/her will, and to the best of our knowledge testator is of legal age to make a will, of sound mind, and under no constraint or undue influence.

_____residing at_____

_____residing at_____

# Last Will and Testament

I, _____ a resident of _____ County, New York do hereby make, publish, and declare this to be my Last Will and Testament, hereby revoking any and all Wills and Codicils heretofore made by me.

FIRST: I direct that all my just debts and funeral expenses be paid out of my estate as soon after my death as is practicable.

SECOND:  I give, devise, and bequeath the following specific gifts:

_____

_____

_____

THIRD: I give, devise, and bequeath the rest, residue and remainder of my estate, real, personal, and mixed, of whatever kind and wherever situated, of which I may die seized or possessed, or in which I may have any interest or over which I may have any power of appointment or testamentary disposition, to my children _____

_____

_____

_____, plus any afterborn or adopted children in equal shares or to their lineal descendants per stirpes.

FOURTH: In the event that any beneficiary fails to survive me by thirty days, then this will shall take effect as if that person had predeceased me.

FIFTH: In the event that any of my children have not reached the age of _____ years at the time of my death, then the share of any such child shall be held in a separate trust by _____ for such child.

The trustee shall use the income and that part of the principal of the trust as is, in the trustee's sole discretion, necessary or desirable to provide proper housing, medical care, food, clothing, entertainment and education for the trust beneficiary, considering the beneficiary's other resources. Any income that is not distributed shall be added to the principal. Additionally, the trustee shall have all powers conferred by the law of the state having jurisdiction over this trust, as well as the power to pay from the assets of the trust reasonable fees necessary to administer the trust.

The trust shall terminate when the child reaches the age specified above and the remaining assets distributed to the child, unless they have been exhausted sooner. In the event the child dies prior to the termination of the trust, then the assets shall pass to the estate of the child. The interests of the beneficiary under this trust shall not be assignable and shall be free from the claims of creditors to the full extent allowed by law.

In the event the said trustee is unable or unwilling to serve for any reason, then I nominate, constitute, and appoint _____as alternate trustee. No bond shall be required of either trustee in any jurisdiction and this trust shall be administered without court supervision as allowed by law.

SIXTH: In the event any of my children have not attained the age of 18 years at the time of my death, I hereby nominate, constitute, and appoint _____ _____as guardian over the person and estate of any of my children who have not reached the age of majority at the time of my death. In the event that said guardian is unable or unwilling to serve, then I nominate, constitute, and appoint _____ as guardian. Said guardian shall serve without bond or surety.

SEVENTH: I hereby nominate, constitute, and appoint _____ _____ as Executor/Executrix of this, my Last Will and Testament. In the event that such named person is unable or unwilling to serve at any time or for any reason, then I nominate, constitute, and appoint _____ as Executor/Executrix in the place and stead of the person first named herein. It is my will and I direct that my Executor/Executrix shall not be required to furnish a bond for the faithful performance of his or her duties in any jurisdiction, any provision of law to the contrary notwithstanding, and I give my Executor/Executrix full power to administer my estate, including the power to settle claims, pay debts, and sell, lease or exchange real and personal property without court order.

IN WITNESS WHEREOF, I declare this to be my Last Will and Testament and execute it willingly as my free and voluntary act for the purposes expressed herein and I am of legal age and sound mind and make this under no constraint or undue influence, this _____ day of _____, _____ at _____ State of _____.

_____L.S.

The foregoing instrument was on said date subscribed at the end thereof by _____, the above named Testator who signed, published, and declared this instrument to be his/her Last Will and Testament in the presence of us and each of us, who thereupon at his/her request, in his/her presence, and in the presence of each other, have hereunto subscribed our names as witnesses thereto. We are of sound mind and proper age to witness a will and understand this to be his/her will, and to the best of our knowledge testator is of legal age to make a will, of sound mind, and under no constraint or undue influence.

_____residing at_____

_____residing at_____

# Last Will and Testament

I, _____ a resident of _____ County, New York do hereby make, publish, and declare this to be my Last Will and Testament, hereby revoking any and all Wills and Codicils heretofore made by me.

FIRST: I direct that all my just debts and funeral expenses be paid out of my estate as soon after my death as is practicable.

SECOND: I give, devise, and bequeath the following specific gifts:

_____
_____
_____

THIRD: I give, devise, and bequeath the rest, residue and remainder of my estate, real, personal, and mixed, of whatever kind and wherever situated, of which I may die seized or possessed, or in which I may have any interest or over which I may have any power of appointment or testamentary disposition, to my children _____

_____
_____
_____,

in equal shares, or their lineal descendants per stirpes.

FOURTH: In the event that any beneficiary fails to survive me by thirty days, then this will shall take effect as if that person had predeceased me.

FIFTH: I hereby nominate, constitute, and appoint _____ _____ as Executor/Executrix of this, my Last Will and Testament. In the event that such named person is unable or unwilling to serve at any time or for any reason, then I nominate, constitute, and appoint _____ as Executor/Executrix in the place and stead of the person first named herein. It is my will and I direct that my Executor/Executrix shall not be required to furnish a bond for the faithful performance of his or her duties in any jurisdiction, any provision of law to the contrary notwithstanding, and I give my Executor/Executrix full power to administer my estate, including the power to settle claims, pay debts, and sell, lease or exchange real and personal property without court order.

IN WITNESS WHEREOF, I declare this to be my Last Will and Testament and execute it willingly as my free and voluntary act for the purposes expressed herein and I am of legal age and sound mind and make this under no constraint or undue influence, this _____ day of _____, _____ at _____ State of _____.

_____L.S.

The foregoing instrument was on said date subscribed at the end thereof by
_____, the above named Testator who signed, published, and declared this instrument to be his/her Last Will and Testament in the presence of us and each of us, who thereupon at his/her request, in his/her presence, and in the presence of each other, have hereunto subscribed our names as witnesses thereto. We are of sound mind and proper age to witness a will and understand this to be his/her will, and to the best of our knowledge testator is of legal age to make a will, of sound mind, and under no constraint or undue influence.

_____residing at_____

_____residing at_____

# Last Will and Testament

I, _____ a resident of _____ County, New York do hereby make, publish, and declare this to be my Last Will and Testament, hereby revoking any and all Wills and Codicils heretofore made by me.

FIRST: I direct that all my just debts and funeral expenses be paid out of my estate as soon after my death as is practicable.

SECOND:  I give, devise, and bequeath the following specific gifts:

_____
_____
_____

THIRD: I give, devise, and bequeath the rest, residue and remainder of my estate, real, personal, and mixed, of whatever kind and wherever situated, of which I may die seized or possessed, or in which I may have any interest or over which I may have any power of appointment or testamentary disposition, to my children _____

_____
_____
_____,

in equal shares, or their lineal descendants per capita.

FOURTH: In the event that any beneficiary fails to survive me by thirty days, then this will shall take effect as if that person had predeceased me.

FIFTH: I hereby nominate, constitute, and appoint _____ _____ as Executor/Executrix of this, my Last Will and Testament. In the event that such named person is unable or unwilling to serve at any time or for any reason, then I nominate, constitute, and appoint _____ as Executor/Executrix in the place and stead of the person first named herein. It is my will and I direct that my Executor/Executrix shall not be required to furnish a bond for the faithful performance of his or her duties in any jurisdiction, any provision of law to the contrary notwithstanding, and I give my Executor/Executrix full power to administer my estate, including the power to settle claims, pay debts, and sell, lease or exchange real and personal property without court order.

IN WITNESS WHEREOF, I declare this to be my Last Will and Testament and execute it willingly as my free and voluntary act for the purposes expressed herein and I am of legal age and sound mind and make this under no constraint or undue influence, this _____ day of _____, _____ at _____ State of _____.

_____L.S.

The foregoing instrument was on said date subscribed at the end thereof by _____, the above named Testator who signed, published, and declared this instrument to be his/her Last Will and Testament in the presence of us and each of us, who thereupon at his/her request, in his/her presence, and in the presence of each other, have hereunto subscribed our names as witnesses thereto. We are of sound mind and proper age to witness a will and understand this to be his/her will, and to the best of our knowledge testator is of legal age to make a will, of sound mind, and under no constraint or undue influence.

_____residing at_____

_____residing at_____

# Last Will and Testament

I, _____ a resident of _____ County, New York do hereby make, publish, and declare this to be my Last Will and Testament, hereby revoking any and all Wills and Codicils heretofore made by me.

FIRST: I direct that all my just debts and funeral expenses be paid out of my estate as soon after my death as is practicable.

SECOND:  I give, devise, and bequeath the following specific gifts:

_____

_____

_____

THIRD: I give, devise, and bequeath the rest, residue and remainder of my estate, real, personal, and mixed, of whatever kind and wherever situated, of which I may die seized or possessed, or in which I may have any interest or over which I may have any power of appointment or testamentary disposition, to the following: _____

_____

_____

_____,

or to the survivor of them.

FOURTH: In the event that any beneficiary fails to survive me by thirty days, then this will shall take effect as if that person had predeceased me.

FIFTH: I hereby nominate, constitute, and appoint _____ as Executor/Executrix of this, my Last Will and Testament. In the event that such named person is unable or unwilling to serve at any time or for any reason, then I nominate, constitute, and appoint _____ as Executor/Executrix in the place and stead of the person first named herein. It is my will and I direct that my Executor/Executrix shall not be required to furnish a bond for the faithful performance of his or her duties in any jurisdiction, any provision of law to the contrary notwithstanding, and I give my Executor/Executrix full power to administer my estate, including the power to settle claims, pay debts, and sell, lease or exchange real and personal property without court order.

IN WITNESS WHEREOF, I declare this to be my Last Will and Testament and execute it willingly as my free and voluntary act for the purposes expressed herein and I am of legal age and sound mind and make this under no constraint or undue influence, this _____ day of _____, _____ at _____ State of _____.

_____L.S.

The foregoing instrument was on said date subscribed at the end thereof by _____, the above named Testator who signed, published, and declared this instrument to be his/her Last Will and Testament in the presence of us and each of us, who thereupon at his/her request, in his/her presence, and in the presence of each other, have hereunto subscribed our names as witnesses thereto. We are of sound mind and proper age to witness a will and understand this to be his/her will, and to the best of our knowledge testator is of legal age to make a will, of sound mind, and under no constraint or undue influence.

_____residing at_____

_____residing at_____

# Last Will and Testament

I, _____ a resident of _____ County, New York do hereby make, publish, and declare this to be my Last Will and Testament, hereby revoking any and all Wills and Codicils heretofore made by me.

FIRST: I direct that all my just debts and funeral expenses be paid out of my estate as soon after my death as is practicable.

SECOND: I give, devise, and bequeath the following specific gifts:

_____

_____

_____

THIRD: I give, devise, and bequeath the rest, residue and remainder of my estate, real, personal, and mixed, of whatever kind and wherever situated, of which I may die seized or possessed, or in which I may have any interest or over which I may have any power of appointment or testamentary disposition, to the following _____

_____

_____

_____,

in equal shares, or their lineal descendants per stirpes.

FOURTH: In the event that any beneficiary fails to survive me by thirty days, then this will shall take effect as if that person had predeceased me.

FIFTH: I hereby nominate, constitute, and appoint _____ _____ as Executor/Executrix of this, my Last Will and Testament. In the event that such named person is unable or unwilling to serve at any time or for any reason, then I nominate, constitute, and appoint _____ as Executor/Executrix in the place and stead of the person first named herein. It is my will and I direct that my Executor/Executrix shall not be required to furnish a bond for the faithful performance of his or her duties in any jurisdiction, any provision of law to the contrary notwithstanding, and I give my Executor/Executrix full power to administer my estate, including the power to settle claims, pay debts, and sell, lease or exchange real and personal property without court order.

IN WITNESS WHEREOF, I declare this to be my Last Will and Testament and execute it willingly as my free and voluntary act for the purposes expressed herein and I am of legal age and sound mind and make this under no constraint or undue influence, this _____ day of _____, _____ at _____ State of _____.

_____L.S.

**95**

The foregoing instrument was on said date subscribed at the end thereof by
_____, the above named Testator who signed, published, and declared this instrument to be his/her Last Will and Testament in the presence of us and each of us, who thereupon at his/her request, in his/her presence, and in the presence of each other, have hereunto subscribed our names as witnesses thereto. We are of sound mind and proper age to witness a will and understand this to be his/her will, and to the best of our knowledge testator is of legal age to make a will, of sound mind, and under no constraint or undue influence.

_____residing at_____

_____residing at_____

# Self-Proved Will Affidavit

(attach to Will)

STATE OF NEW YORK

COUNTY OF _____

Each of the undersigned, individually and severally being duly sworn deposes and says:

The within will was subscribed in our presence and sight at the end thereof by _____, the within named testat_____, on the _____ day of _____, _____, at _____ o'clock.

Said testat____ at the time of making such subscription declared the instrument so subscribed to be h___ last will.

Each of the undersigned thereupon signed h___ name as a witness at the end of said will at the request of said testat_____ and in h___ presence and sight and in the presence and sight of each other.

Said testat_____ was, at the time of so executing said will, over the age of 18 years and, in the respective opinions of the undersigned, of sound mind, memory and understanding and not under any restraint or in any respect incompetent to make a will.

The testat_____, in the respective opinions of the undersigned, could read, write and converse in the English language and was suffering from no defect of sight, hearing or speech, or from any other physical or mental impairment which would affect h___ capacity to make a valid will. The will was executed as a single, original instrument and was not executed in counterparts.

Each of the undersigned was acquainted with said testat_____ at such time and makes this affidavit at h___ request.

The within will was shown to the undersigned at the time this affidavit was made, and was examined by each of them as to the signature of said testat_____ and of the undersigned.

_____ (Witness)

_____ (Witness)

Subscribed, sworn and acknowledged before me by _____, the testator, and by _____ and _____ _____, witnesses, this _____ day of _____.

_____

Notary or other officer

# Codicil to the Will of

_____

I, _____, a resident of _____ County, New York declare this to be the first codicil to my Last Will and Testament dated _____, _____.

FIRST: I hereby revoke the clause of my Will which reads as follows:

_____

_____

_____

_____.

SECOND: I hereby add the following clause to my Will: _____

_____

_____

_____.

THIRD: In all other respects I hereby confirm and republish my Last Will and Testament dated _____, _____.

IN WITNESS WHEREOF, I have signed, published, and declared the foregoing instrument as and for a codicil to my Last Will and Testament, this _____ day of _____, _____.

_____

The foregoing instrument was on the _____ day of _____, _____, signed at the end thereof, and at the same time published and declared by _____, as and for a codicil to his/her Last Will and Testament, dated _____, _____, in the presence of each of us, who, this attestation clause having been read to us, did at the request of the said testator/testatrix, in his/her presence and in the presence of each other signed our names as witnesses thereto.

_____residing at_____

_____residing at_____

# Self-Proved Codicil Affidavit
### (attach to Codicil)

STATE OF NEW YORK

COUNTY OF _____

Each of the undersigned, individually and severally being duly sworn deposes and says:

The within codicil was subscribed in our presence and sight at the end thereof by _____, the within named testat_____, on the _____ day of _____, _____, at _____o'clock.

Said testat____ at the time of making such subscription declared the instrument so subscribed to be h____ last codicil to h__ last will.

Each of the undersigned thereupon signed h____ name as a witness at the end of said codicil at the request of said testat____ and in h__ presence and sight and in the presence and sight of each other.

Said testat____ was, at the time of so executing said will (codicil), over the age of 18 years and, in the respective opinions of the undersigned, of sound mind, memory and understanding and not under any restraint or in any respect incompetent to make a codicil.

The testat____, in the respective opinions of the undersigned, could read, write and converse in the English language and was suffering from no defect of sight, hearing or speech, or from any other physical or mental impairment which would affect h__ capacity to make a valid codicil. The codicil was executed as a single, original instrument and was not executed in counterparts.

Each of the undersigned was acquainted with said testat____ at such time and makes this affidavit at h__ request.

The within codicil was shown to the undersigned at the time this affidavit was made, and was examined by each of them as to the signature of said testat____ and of the undersigned.

_____(Witness)

_____(Witness)

Subscribed, sworn and acknowledged before me by _____, the testator, and by _____ and _____ _____, witnesses, this _____ day of _____.

_____
Notary or other officer

# Living Will

Declaration made this ____ day of _____, _____. I, _____, willfully and voluntarily make known my desire that my dying not be artificially prolonged under the circumstances set forth below, and I do hereby declare:

If at any time I have a terminal condition and if my attending or treating physician and another consulting physician have determined that there can be no medical probability of my recovery from such condition, I direct that life-prolonging procedures be withheld or withdrawn when the application of such procedures would serve only to prolong artificially the process of dying, and that I be permitted to die naturally with only the administration of medication or the performance of any medical procedure deemed necessary to provide me with comfort, care or alleviate pain.

It is my intention that this declaration be honored by my family and physician as the final expression of my legal right to refuse medical or surgical treatment and to accept the consequences for such refusal.

This authorization includes ( ) does not include ( ) the withholding or withdrawal of artificial feeding and hydration (Check only one box above).

Special Instructions (if any) _____
_____
_____

Signed this ____ day of _____, _____.

_____
Signature
Address:_____
_____

I understand the full import of this declaration, and am emotionally and mentally competent to make this declaration.

Additional instructions (optional):

_____
_____

_____
(Signed)

_____     _____
Witness                              Witness

_____     _____
Address                              Address

_____     _____
Phone                                Phone

**UNIFORM DONOR CARD**

The undersigned hereby makes this anatomical gift, if medically acceptable, to take effect on death. The words and marks below indicate my desires:

I give:

(a) ____ any needed organs or parts;

(b) ____ only the following organs or parts

_____

for the purpose of transplantation, therapy, medical research, or education;

(c) ____ my body for anatomical study if needed.

Limitations or special wishes, if any:

_____

Signed by the donor and the following witnesses in the presence of each other:

_____    _____
Signature of Donor              Date of birth

_____    _____
Date signed                      City & State

_____    _____
Witness                          Witness

_____    _____
Address                          Address

---

**UNIFORM DONOR CARD**

The undersigned hereby makes this anatomical gift, if medically acceptable, to take effect on death. The words and marks below indicate my desires:

I give:

(a) ____ any needed organs or parts;

(b) ____ only the following organs or parts

_____

for the purpose of transplantation, therapy, medical research, or education;

(c) ____ my body for anatomical study if needed.

Limitations or special wishes, if any:

_____

Signed by the donor and the following witnesses in the presence of each other:

_____    _____
Signature of Donor              Date of birth

_____    _____
Date signed                      City & State

_____    _____
Witness                          Witness

_____    _____
Address                          Address

---

**UNIFORM DONOR CARD**

The undersigned hereby makes this anatomical gift, if medically acceptable, to take effect on death. The words and marks below indicate my desires:

I give:

(a) ____ any needed organs or parts;

(b) ____ only the following organs or parts

_____

for the purpose of transplantation, therapy, medical research, or education;

(c) ____ my body for anatomical study if needed.

Limitations or special wishes, if any:

_____

Signed by the donor and the following witnesses in the presence of each other:

_____    _____
Signature of Donor              Date of birth

_____    _____
Date signed                      City & State

_____    _____
Witness                          Witness

_____    _____
Address                          Address

---

**UNIFORM DONOR CARD**

The undersigned hereby makes this anatomical gift, if medically acceptable, to take effect on death. The words and marks below indicate my desires:

I give:

(a) ____ any needed organs or parts;

(b) ____ only the following organs or parts

_____

for the purpose of transplantation, therapy, medical research, or education;

(c) ____ my body for anatomical study if needed.

Limitations or special wishes, if any:

_____

Signed by the donor and the following witnesses in the presence of each other:

_____    _____
Signature of Donor              Date of birth

_____    _____
Date signed                      City & State

_____    _____
Witness                          Witness

_____    _____
Address                          Address

One of these cards should be cut out and carried in your wallet or purse.

# GLOSSARY

**administrator** (*administratrix* if female). A person appointed by the court to oversee distribution of the property of someone who died (either without a will, or if the person designated in the will is unable to serve).

**attested will**. A will which includes an attestation clause and has been signed in front of witnesses.

**beneficiary**. A person who is entitled to receive property from a person who died (regardless of whether there is a will).

**bequest**. Personal property left to someone in a will.

**children's trust**. A trust set up to hold property given to children. Usually it provides that the children will not receive their property until they reach a higher age than the age of majority.

**codicil**. An amendment to a will.

**community property**. Property acquired by a husband and wife by their labors during their marriage.

**decedent**. A person who has died.

**descendent**. A child, grandchild, great-grandchild, etc.

**devise**. Real property left to someone in a will. A person who is entitled to a devise is called a *devisee*.

**elective share.** In non-community property states, the portion of the estate which may be taken by a surviving spouse, regardless of what the will says.

**executor** (*executrix* if female). A person appointed in a will to oversee distribution of the property of someone who died with a will.

**exempt property.** Property that is exempt from distribution as a normal part of the estate.

**family allowance.** An amount of money set aside from the estate to support the family of the decedent for a period of time.

**forced share.** *See* **elective share**.

**heir.** A person who will inherit from a decedent who died without a will.

**holographic will.** A will in which all of the material provisions are entirely in the handwriting on the maker. Holographic wills are not legal if not witnessed.

**intestate.** Without making a will. One who dies without a will is said to have *died intestate*.

**intestate share.** In non-community property states, the portion of the estate a spouse is entitled to receive if there is no will.

**joint tenancy.** A type of property ownership by two or more persons, in which if one owner dies, that owner's interest goes to the other joint tenants (not to the deceased owner's heirs as in tenancy in common).

**legacy.** Real property left to someone in a will. A person who is entitled to a legacy is called a *legatee*.

**living will.** A document expressing the writer's desires regarding how medical care is to be handled in the event the writer is not able to express his or her wishes concerning the use of life-prolonging medical procedures.

**per capita.** Distribution of property with equal shares going to each person.

**per stirpes.** Distribution of property with equal shares going to each family line.

**personal representative.** A person appointed by the court, or will, to oversee distribution of the property of the person who died. This is a more modern term than "administrator," "executor," etc., and applies regardless of whether there is a will.

**probate**. The process of settling a decedent's estate through the probate court.

**residue**. The property that is left over in an estate after all specific bequests and devises.

**self-proving affidavit**. A form added to a will in which the will maker and witnesses state under oath that they have signed and witnessed the will.

**specific bequest** *or* **specific devise**. A gift in a will of a specific item of property, or a specific amount of cash.

**statutory will**. A will which has been prepared according to the requirements of a statute.

**tenancy by the entirety**. A type of property ownership by a married couple, in which the property automatically passes to one spouse upon the death of the other. This is basically the same as joint tenancy, except that it is only between a husband and wife.

**tenancy in common**. Ownership of property by two or more people, in which each owner's share would descend to that owner's heirs (not to the other owners as in joint tenancy).

**testate**. With a will. One who dies with a will is said to have *died testate*.

**testator**. (*testatrix* if female.) A person who makes his or her will.

**testamentary substitute**. The giving away of property during a person's life in the form of joint tenancies, revocable trusts or gifts, in order to avoid his/her spouse receiving an elective share.

# INDEX

*Your #1 Source for Real World Legal Information...*

# SPHINX® PUBLISHING
## A Division of Sourcebooks, Inc.®
- Written by lawyers
- Simple English explanation of the law
- Forms and instructions included

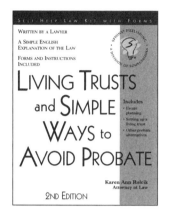

NEW YORK POWER OF ATTORNEY
HANDBOOK

Provides information concerning
New York's power of attorney
laws. It also explains when and
why you need power of attorney.
Includes forms.

138 pages; $19.95;
ISBN 1-57071-188-7

HOW TO FILE FOR DIVORCE IN
NEW YORK

A simple guide for obtaining a
divorce in New York. This book provides essential information concerning property division, grounds for
divorce, child custody issues and
more. Includes forms to file with
insructions.

May
ISBN 1-57248-064-5

LIVING TRUSTS AND SIMPLE WAYS TO
AVOID PROBATE, 2ND ED.

This book explains what probate is,
the advantages and disadvantages of
probate and more. Provides information on alternatives to probate,
including: joint ownership, life insurance and land trusts. Includes necessary forms to file plus instructions.

166 pages; $19.95;
ISBN 1-57071-336-7

See the following order form for books written specifically for California,
Florida, Georgia, Illinois, Massachusetts, Michigan, Minnesota, New York,
North Carolina, Pennsylvania, and Texas! *Coming soon—Ohio and New Jersey!*

*What our customers say about our books:*

"It couldn't be more clear for the lay person." —R.D.

"I want you to know I really appreciate your book.  It has saved me a lot of time and money." —L.T.

"Your real estate contracts book has saved me nearly $12,000.00 in closing costs over the past year." —A.B.

"...many of the legal questions that I have had over the years were answered clearly and concisely
through your plain English interpretation of the law." —C.E.H.

"If there weren't people out there like you I'd be lost.  You have the best books of this type out there." —S.B.

"...your forms and directions are easy to follow." —C.V.M.

*Sphinx Publishing's Legal Survival Guides*
*are directly available from the Sourcebooks, Inc., or from your local bookstores.*
*For credit card orders call 1–800–43–BRIGHT, write P.O. Box 372, Naperville, IL 60566,*
*or fax 630-961-2168*

# SPHINX® PUBLISHING'S NATIONAL TITLES
## *Valid in All 50 States*

### LEGAL SURVIVAL IN BUSINESS

| | |
|---|---|
| How to Form a Limited Liability Company (April) | $19.95 |
| How to Form Your Own Corporation (2E) | $19.95 |
| How to Form Your Own Partnership | $19.95 |
| How to Register Your Own Copyright (2E) | $19.95 |
| How to Register Your Own Trademark (2E) | $19.95 |
| Most Valuable Business Legal Forms You'll Ever Need (2E) | $19.95 |
| Most Valuable Corporate Forms You'll Ever Need (2E) | $24.95 |
| Software Law (with diskette) | $29.95 |

### LEGAL SURVIVAL IN COURT

| | |
|---|---|
| Crime Victim's Guide to Justice | $19.95 |
| Debtors' Rights (3E) | $12.95 |
| Defend Yourself against Criminal Charges | $19.95 |
| Grandparents' Rights (2E) | $19.95 |
| Help Your Lawyer Win Your Case | $12.95 |
| Jurors' Rights (2E) | $9.95 |
| Legal Malpractice and Other Claims against Your Lawyer (2E) (June) | $18.95 |
| Legal Research Made Easy (2E) | $14.95 |
| Simple Ways to Protect Yourself from Lawsuits | $24.95 |
| Victims' Rights | $12.95 |
| Winning Your Personal Injury Claim | $19.95 |

### LEGAL SURVIVAL IN REAL ESTATE

| | |
|---|---|
| How to Buy a Condominium or Townhome | $16.95 |
| How to Negotiate Real Estate Contracts (3E) | $16.95 |
| How to Negotiate Real Estate Leases (3E) | $16.95 |
| Successful Real Estate Brokerage Management | $19.95 |

### LEGAL SURVIVAL IN PERSONAL AFFAIRS

| | |
|---|---|
| How to File Your Own Bankruptcy (4E) | $19.95 |
| How to File Your Own Divorce (3E) | $19.95 |
| How to Make Your Own Will | $12.95 |
| How to Write Your Own Living Will | $9.95 |
| How to Write Your Own Premarital Agreement (2E) | $19.95 |
| How to Win Your Unemployment Compensation Claim | $19.95 |
| Living Trusts and Simple Ways to Avoid Probate (2E) | $19.95 |
| Neighbors' Rights | $12.95 |
| The Power of Attorney Handbook (3E) | $19.95 |
| Simple Ways to Protect Yourself from Lawsuits | $24.95 |
| Social Security Benefits Handbook (2E) | $14.95 |
| Unmarried Parents' Rights | $19.95 |
| U.S.A. Immigration Guide (3E) | $19.95 |
| Guia de Inmigracion a Estados Unidos (2E) (May) | $19.95 |

*Legal Survival Guides are directly available from Sourcebooks, Inc., or from your local bookstores.*

*For credit card orders call 1–800–43–BRIGHT, write P.O. Box 372, Naperville, IL 60566,
or fax 630-961-2168*

# SPHINX® PUBLISHING ORDER FORM

| BILL TO: | | SHIP TO: | |
|---|---|---|---|
| | | | |
| | | | |
| Phone # | Terms | F.O.B. Chicago, IL | Ship Date |

**Charge my:** ☐ VISA    ☐ MasterCard    ☐ American Express

☐ **Money Order or Personal Check**

Credit Card Number [ ][ ][ ][ ][ ][ ][ ][ ][ ][ ][ ][ ][ ][ ][ ][ ]    Expiration Date [ ][ ][ ][ ]

| Qty | ISBN | Title | Retail | Ext. |
|---|---|---|---|---|
| | | **SPHINX PUBLISHING NATIONAL TITLES** | | |
| | 1-57071-166-6 | Crime Victim's Guide to Justice | $19.95 | |
| | 1-57071-342-1 | Debtors' Rights (3E) | $12.95 | |
| | 1-57071-162-3 | Defend Yourself against Criminal Charges | $19.95 | |
| | 1-57248-082-3 | Grandparents' Rights (2E) | $19.95 | |
| | 1-57248-087-4 | Guia de Inmigracion a Estados Unidos (2E) (May) | $19.95 | |
| | 1-57248-021-1 | Help Your Lawyer Win Your Case | $12.95 | |
| | 1-57071-164-X | How to Buy a Condominium or Townhome | $16.95 | |
| | 1-57071-223-9 | How to File Your Own Bankruptcy (4E) | $19.95 | |
| | 1-57071-224-7 | How to File Your Own Divorce (3E) | $19.95 | |
| | 1-57248-083-1 | How to Form a Limited Liability Company (April) | $19.95 | |
| | 1-57071-227-1 | How to Form Your Own Corporation (2E) | $19.95 | |
| | 1-57071-343-X | How to Form Your Own Partnership | $19.95 | |
| | 1-57071-228-X | How to Make Your Own Will | $12.95 | |
| | 1-57071-331-6 | How to Negotiate Real Estate Contracts (3E) | $16.95 | |
| | 1-57071-332-4 | How to Negotiate Real Estate Leases (3E) | $16.95 | |
| | 1-57071-225-5 | How to Register Your Own Copyright (2E) | $19.95 | |
| | 1-57071-226-3 | How to Register Your Own Trademark (2E) | $19.95 | |
| | 1-57071-349-9 | How to Win Your Unemployment Compensation Claim | $19.95 | |
| | 1-57071-167-4 | How to Write Your Own Living Will | $9.95 | |
| | 1-57071-344-8 | How to Write Your Own Premarital Agreement (2E) | $19.95 | |
| | 1-57071-333-2 | Jurors' Rights (2E) | $9.95 | |
| | 1-57248-090-4 | Legal Malpractice and Other Claims against....(2E) (June) | $18.95 | |
| | 1-57071-400-2 | Legal Research Made Easy (2E) | $14.95 | |
| | 1-57071-336-7 | Living Trusts and Simple Ways to Avoid Probate (2E) | $19.95 | |
| | 1-57071-345-6 | Most Valuable Bus. Legal Forms You'll Ever Need (2E) | $19.95 | |
| | 1-57071-346-4 | Most Valuable Corporate Forms You'll Ever Need (2E) | $24.95 | |
| | 1-57248-089-0 | Neighbors' Rights | $12.95 | |
| | 1-57071-348-0 | The Power of Attorney Handbook (3E) | $19.95 | |
| | 1-57248-020-3 | Simple Ways to Protect Yourself from Lawsuits | $24.95 | |
| | 1-57071-337-5 | Social Security Benefits Handbook (2E) | $14.95 | |
| | 1-57071-163-1 | Software Law (w/diskette) | $29.95 | |
| | 0-913825-86-7 | Successful Real Estate Brokerage Mgmt. | $19.95 | |
| | 1-57071-399-5 | Unmarried Parents' Rights | $19.95 | |
| | 1-57071-354-5 | U.S.A. Immigration Guide (3E) | $19.95 | |
| | 0-913825-82-4 | Victims' Rights | $12.95 | |
| | 1-57071-165-8 | Winning Your Personal Injury Claim | $19.95 | |
| | | **CALIFORNIA TITLES** | | |
| | 1-57071-360-X | CA Power of Attorney Handbook | $12.95 | |
| | 1-57071-355-3 | How to File for Divorce in CA | $19.95 | |
| | 1-57071-356-1 | How to Make a CA Will | $12.95 | |
| | 1-57071-408-8 | How to Probate an Estate in CA (April) | $19.95 | |
| | 1-57071-357-X | How to Start a Business in CA | $16.95 | |
| | 1-57071-358-8 | How to Win in Small Claims Court in CA | $14.95 | |
| | 1-57071-359-6 | Landlords' Rights and Duties in CA | $19.95 | |
| | | **FLORIDA TITLES** | | |
| | 1-57071-363-4 | Florida Power of Attorney Handbook (2E) | $12.95 | |
| | 1-57248-093-9 | How to File for Divorce in FL (6E) (July) | $21.95 | |
| | 1-57248-086-6 | How to Form a Limited Liability Co. in FL (April) | $19.95 | |
| | 1-57071-401-0 | How to Form a Partnership in FL | $19.95 | |
| | 1-57071-380-4 | How to Form a Corporation in FL (4E) | $19.95 | |
| | 1-57071-361-8 | How to Make a FL Will (5E) | $12.95 | |
| | 1-57248-088-2 | How to Modify Your FL Divorce Judgement (4E)(May) | $22.95 | |
| | **Form Continued on Following Page** | | **SUBTOTAL** | |

To order, call Sourcebooks at 1-800-43-BRIGHT or FAX (630)961-2168 (Bookstores, libraries, wholesalers—please call for discount)

# SPHINX® PUBLISHING ORDER FORM

| Qty | ISBN | Title | Retail | Ext. |
|-----|------|-------|--------|------|
| | | **FLORIDA TITLES (CONT'D)** | | |
| ____ | 1-57071-364-2 | How to Probate an Estate in FL (3E) | $24.95 | ____ |
| ____ | 1-57248-081-5 | How to Start a Business in FL (5E) (March) | $16.95 | ____ |
| ____ | 1-57071-362-6 | How to Win in Small Claims Court in FL (6E) | $14.95 | ____ |
| ____ | 1-57071-335-9 | Landlords' Rights and Duties in FL (7E) | $19.95 | ____ |
| ____ | 1-57071-334-0 | Land Trusts in FL (5E) | $24.95 | ____ |
| ____ | 0-913825-73-5 | Women's Legal Rights in FL | $19.95 | ____ |
| | | **GEORGIA TITLES** | | |
| ____ | 1-57071-376-6 | How to File for Divorce in GA (3E) | $19.95 | ____ |
| ____ | 1-57248-075-0 | How to Make a GA Will (3E) | $12.95 | ____ |
| ____ | 1-57248-076-9 | How to Start a Business in Georgia (3E) | $16.95 | ____ |
| | | **ILLINOIS TITLES** | | |
| ____ | 1-57071-405-3 | How to File for Divorce in IL (2E) | $19.95 | ____ |
| ____ | 1-57071-415-0 | How to Make an IL Will (2E) | $12.95 | ____ |
| ____ | 1-57071-416-9 | How to Start a Business in IL (2E) | $16.95 | ____ |
| ____ | 1-57248-078-5 | Landlords' Rights & Duties in IL (February) | $19.95 | ____ |
| | | **MASSACHUSETTS TITLES** | | |
| ____ | 1-57071-329-4 | How to File for Divorce in MA (2E) | $19.95 | ____ |
| ____ | 1-57248-050-5 | How to Make a MA Will | $9.95 | ____ |
| ____ | 1-57248-053-X | How to Probate an Estate in MA | $19.95 | ____ |
| ____ | 1-57248-054-8 | How to Start a Business in MA | $16.95 | ____ |
| ____ | 1-57248-055-6 | Landlords' Rights and Duties in MA | $19.95 | ____ |
| | | **MICHIGAN TITLES** | | |
| ____ | 1-57071-409-6 | How to File for Divorce in MI (2E) | $19.95 | ____ |
| ____ | 1-57248-077-7 | How to Make a MI Will (2E) | $12.95 | ____ |
| ____ | 1-57071-407-X | How to Start a Business in MI (2E) | $16.95 | ____ |
| | | **MINNESOTA TITLES** | | |
| ____ | 1-57248-039-4 | How to File for Divorce in MN | $19.95 | ____ |
| ____ | 1-57248-040-8 | How to Form a Simple Corporation in MN | $19.95 | ____ |
| ____ | 1-57248-037-8 | How to Make a MN Will | $9.95 | ____ |
| ____ | 1-57248-038-6 | How to Start a Business in MN | $16.95 | ____ |
| | | **NEW YORK TITLES** | | |

| Qty | ISBN | Title | Retail | Ext. |
|-----|------|-------|--------|------|
| ____ | 1-57071-184-4 | How to File for Divorce in NY (March) | $19.95 | ____ |
| ____ | 1-57248-095-5 | How to Make a NY Will (2E) | $12.95 | ____ |
| ____ | 1-57071-185-2 | How to Start a Business in NY | $16.95 | ____ |
| ____ | 1-57071-187-9 | How to Win in Small Claims Court in NY | $14.95 | ____ |
| ____ | 1-57071-186-0 | Landlords' Rights and Duties in NY (March) | $19.95 | ____ |
| ____ | 1-57071-188-7 | New York Power of Attorney Handbook | $19.95 | ____ |
| | | **NORTH CAROLINA TITLES** | | |
| ____ | 1-57071-326-X | How to File for Divorce in NC (2E) | $19.95 | ____ |
| ____ | 1-57071-327-8 | How to Make a NC Will (2E) | $12.95 | ____ |
| ____ | 1-57248-096-3 | How to Start a Business in NC (2E) | $16.95 | ____ |
| ____ | 1-57248-091-2 | Landlords' Rights & Duties in NC (June) | $19.95 | ____ |
| | | **PENNSYLVANIA TITLES** | | |
| ____ | 1-57071-177-1 | How to File for Divorce in PA | $19.95 | ____ |
| ____ | 1-57248-094-7 | How to Make a PA Will (2E) | $12.95 | ____ |
| ____ | 1-57071-178-X | How to Start a Business in PA | $16.95 | ____ |
| ____ | 1-57071-179-8 | Landlords' Rights and Duties in PA (June) | $19.95 | ____ |
| | | **TEXAS TITLES** | | |
| ____ | 1-57071-330-8 | How to File for Divorce in TX (2E) | $19.95 | ____ |
| ____ | 1-57248-009-2 | How to Form a Simple Corporation in TX | $19.95 | ____ |
| ____ | 1-57071-417-7 | How to Make a TX Will (2E) | $12.95 | ____ |
| ____ | 1-57071-418-5 | How to Probate an Estate in TX (2E) | $19.95 | ____ |
| ____ | 1-57071-365-0 | How to Start a Business in TX (2E) | $16.95 | ____ |
| ____ | 1-57248-012-2 | How to Win in Small Claims Court in TX | $14.95 | ____ |
| ____ | 1-57248-011-4 | Landlords' Rights and Duties in TX | $19.95 | ____ |

**SUBTOTAL THIS PAGE** _____

**SUBTOTAL PREVIOUS PAGE** _____

Illinois residents add 6.75% sales tax

Florida residents add 6% state sales tax plus applicable discretionary surtax _____

Shipping— $4.00 for 1st book, $1.00 each additional _____

**TOTAL** _____